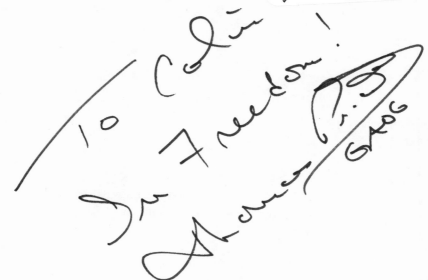

Saving The American Miracle

The Destruction and Restoration of
American Values

Rep. Tom Price M.D.

L. Gerald Davis

Hold on, my friends, to the Constitution and to the Republic for which it stands. Miracles do not cluster, and what has happened once in 6000 years, may not happen again. Hold on to the Constitution, for if the American Constitution should fail, there will be anarchy throughout the world.
--- Daniel Webster

Library of Congress Control Number: 2010917500

ISBN - 10: 1456365460
ISBN - 13: 978-1456365462

Published in the United States of America

I thank God for the blessing of heritage which gave me the gifts of a fighting spirit, an unwavering optimism, supreme confidence, and patriotic love. Dedication of this work goes to my fearless wife, Betty, who is a remarkable source of enthusiasm, strength, principle, and conviction, who palpably loves freedom and who has been my steadfast partner in our walk of faith and service - and, most especially, to our progeny, our son, Robert, his generation and those to come, who must embrace the torch of liberty and protect it.

Special thanks to Bryan Clark, my brother-in-law, who, having lived both in the United States and not, has a keen perspective on and love for liberty, and who was invaluable in his proof-reading and suggestions on the multiple drafts of this work. --- TEP

This book is dedicated to my wife, Nancy. Without her inspiration and encouragement, it would not have been written. It is also dedicated to Ashley and Christopher (and to any grandchildren as yet unborn). May the country they inherit continue to be a bastion of freedom and stand as a "city upon a hill". --- LGD

Contents

Preamble

I love my country. I am an unabashed patriot. I believe that we are blessed to be living in a Constitutional Republic that is the most amazing, the most successful experiment in government ever invented by the human race.

This nation, our nation, the United States of America, is not just a system of government. It is the history of a people. It is a history that begins with the love of freedom. So great was that love, that our founders pursued their quest while risking "their lives, their fortunes and their sacred honor". It is the history of a young nation under an evil suppression from distant shores. It is the history of blood, shed in a great struggle to achieve what is fundamentally good for *all* its peoples. It is the history of a small group of independent states, who ultimately mended wounds, bound together, and emerged strongly united, the strongest on earth.

Our nation is not just a government. It is a fragile dream that recognizes the inherent God-given right of every citizen to "life, liberty and the pursuit of happiness". This dream became reality as our Constitutional framework transformed us into a unified land. The dream became a solid foundation for a people who, protected by these "unalienable" rights, achieved the most spectacular progress in every human endeavor that the world has ever seen.

Our nation is not just a government. It is a legacy of hard work, diligence, perseverance, creativity and unbounded achievement. It is a legacy of vigilance, sacrifice, courage and triumph over daunting challenges. It is a legacy of defending freedom. It is a legacy of American character. We, the people, have inherited this precious gift, and we must guard and preserve it for our posterity.

Our nation is not just a government. It is a system of values, principles and ideals, forged by our founders, embraced by both leaders and citizens throughout our history, and handed down from generation to generation. Being a nation managed by imperfect human beings, we have made mistakes and sometimes fallen short of these original ideals. Yet these foundational beliefs have guided us to become a beacon of political freedom and economic opportunity to the entire world. These values have blessed our nation as we have become the strongest, most productive, the richest and consequently the most generous and merciful nation that has ever existed.

I love my country, but I now fear and distrust what my government has become.

Our founding principles and ideals still exist within individual citizens, but they are rapidly eroding as the cornerstone upon which our federal government functions. In many instances, the actions of the branches of our federal government actually discriminate against the very principles and values that defined us as America for two centuries. Because the federal government now controls or influences virtually every aspect of our lives, this may be a harbinger of whether individuals who cherish these principles can survive under the mandates of such a government.

Since the New Deal of the 1930's, our nation has moved toward a totalitarian state.[1]   Sometimes, slowly and gradually, sometimes, in economic crisis or military peril, more rapidly.   But always, inexorably, toward more laws, more regulation, more control, more programs, more bureaucracies, more spending, more entitlements, more largesse, and more confiscation of personal wealth and property to pay for it all. This has inevitably resulted in individuals and private entities enjoying less freedom and exercising less personal responsibility.   Our federal government, whether led by Republicans or Democrats, has become overbearingly paternalistic, ready to solve every "problem", react to every "crisis", and protect every person from every "peril", whether self-imposed, accidental or imagined. It even attempts to protect us from having our feelings hurt.

Bluntly stated, there has been a vacuum of principled, Conservative, patriotic leadership in our country for decades.   We have strayed from electing national politicians who govern according to traditional American rights and values. Moreover, the American people have been blind or complacent in recognizing the insidious march towards totalitarianism. Have we been blinded by political rhetoric? Have we been softened by the amazing economic blessings our country has provided? Certainly some have become addicted to government largesse. Regardless, we all share blame.

There is another, very apt description of this federal, totalitarian paternalism...it is called tyranny. Mark R. Levin accurately and superbly explains this condition in his bestseller, *Liberty and Tyranny.* [2] Obviously, our federal government does not exercise the brutal, dictatorial tyranny of a North Korea or Zimbabwe; at least, not yet. Nevertheless, it is an insidious form of tyranny. Alexis de Tocqueville, a prophetic political thinker of the 19th century, called it a "soft tyranny"[3]. Regardless of whether brutal or soft, it is dividing our nation.

Some people in our country vehemently embrace "social democracy" and "social justice". They believe that a paternalistic, totalitarian government is the best way to achieve these goals, and satisfy the needs and desires of the people. They believe that capitalism is inherently unfair and that redistribution of wealth is a just outcome. They believe an elite ruling class, using money confiscated from the productive class, can best provide equality for the masses. They believe that every person in this country has a "right" to be cared for. They believe that reliance on and obedience to the state is essential. They believe that God has become irrelevant.

However, a growing number of Americans recognize and reject this tyranny. These brave citizens embrace the principles of freedom, personal responsibility, strength of character, and achievement based on merit. They adhere to freedom of thought and expression, and the freedom of worship. They want the freedom of equal opportunity without the meddling guarantee of equal outcomes. They believe in their hearts that the totalitarian path will ultimately be disastrous for our country. They know historically it has failed every time it has ascended to usurp power from the people. They understand all too well how it leads to dissolution of the state, sacking of enterprise, corruption of society, and, in the end, misery for the people. I firmly believe that the majority of

Americans who appreciate our heritage are well aware of this danger.

How do we reconcile this as a nation? How do we turn this tide of "neo-totalitarianism" and begin a restoration of foundational American principles and ideals? How do we rekindle the passion for freedom that started this great national experiment 234 years ago?

Let us begin with a glimpse into the future.

The family you are about to meet lives in a country that you will not recognize. This country is not a foreign, fictional or make-believe place. This country is the United States of America as it might become in a very few years. This prediction is not a fantasy; it is a looming reality. The stated goals of our current governing elite and the rapid, almost exponential speed with which these goals are being achieved, permits us to envision such a future.

Our Summer Vacation -- August 2029

This summer, I took my wife and two children camping through the Western United States. We had saved for a special trip for a couple of years, and the children were anxious to get out of our apartment complex and see "some new stuff". My wife and I both are given 12 weeks of vacation from our jobs in the U.S. Department of Consumer Banking (she is a teller and I am an assistant branch manager), but we just don't have enough surplus after taxes to do much travel, or really anything extraordinary. I guess we should really be grateful, since our federal tax rate is only 48%. Many working families pay much more. All of us lucky working folks are pretty much in the same boat of "getting by with a little left over".

I guess I should explain why I consider myself "lucky". Unemployment in the U.S. has risen gradually but steadily since the Great Recession of 2008-2014. Only about 65% of our 450 million people have jobs. Roughly 160 million folks either cannot find jobs or simply do not want to work. Our government has spent trillions of dollars on programs to stimulate private job creation, but our nation's businesses just will not step up to the plate and hire. They keep whining about job-killing taxes, health care penalties and stifling regulations, but we know (because the TV tells us) that they are just keeping more of their profits for themselves instead of giving jobs to deserving people.

Fortunately, our government has protected the folks. Governments at all levels provide about 30% of the good jobs in our country. And thankfully, federal programs make sure that the 160 million who don't work have a modest income, healthy food, a clean, safe place to live, and complete medical care.

We had originally planned on a trip for five, but, sadly, our youngest child Heather passed away last April. Heather was born with severe birth defects. Even though the Federal Board of Health Care (FBHC) guidelines strongly recommended that we abort her when the mandatory pre-natal MRI revealed the defects, we just could not do it. Today, we would no longer have that option, but back then, we still had the choice. After five years of treatment, the FBHC regulations prohibited more care because she had exceeded her fair allotment of medical resources. The good news is that the FBHC paid for everything, so we were still able to take our vacation.

After Heather died, my wife and I no longer had to share our bedroom with her. The National Fair Housing

Authority has assigned us a two-bedroom apartment, but we desperately want our own house. We have been on the NFHA home purchase waiting list for four years, but there are only so many single-family houses available these days. Environmental laws protecting every species of plant, tree and animal, plus the federal Sustainable Growth legislation that limits each citizen's carbon footprint has restricted the amount of land and materials devoted to building individual houses. Because the "Baby Boomers" are for the most part still living in their homes, and because there has been such a huge increase in the population from us "Millennials" having children and from the explosion of immigrant families, the country has been in a housing shortage for 15 years.

The NFHA program that we are waiting for qualifies us for a no-down-payment, low-interest mortgage. We certainly cannot afford the 27% interest for a private mortgage loan. Those unregulated interest rates are incredible, but as I understand it, are driven by our current hyperinflation. The TV pundits say the inflation is caused by the size of our Patriotic National Debt (which is now about $42 Trillion) and the resulting weakness of the dollar. We'll just wait for our government loan money.

The good news is that because our NFHA apartment is subsidized, we can afford luxuries like traveling in our own car. We consider it a luxury because gasoline costs $18.50 per gallon. Even with aggressive MPG standards on foreign carmakers (and of course the U.S. Department of Automobile Production, which makes Chevrolets and Chryslers, has rigid fuel efficiency regulations), our domestic supply of gasoline has become scarce. I guess this is due to the environmental prohibition on drilling for and refining oil in this country. All our gasoline is refined in Mexico, Central America and India and then imported.

In 2015, the Middle East War between Israel and Iran, which included tactical nuclear strikes on both sides, devastated middle-eastern oil production and shipping for years, and drove the price of crude sky high. Oh, and one other thing, federal and state gasoline taxes total 53% to help fund our national health care system.

We considered renting an electric car. The federal Department of Transportation, using funds from the 2019 Stimulus Recovery Act, built and operates thousands of charging stations all over the country to encourage the public to try electric driving, but the electricity to charge the cars costs 35 cents per kilowatt-hour. Wow, I remember my Mom telling me that electricity was about 8 cents per kWh in 2008. Back then, they could afford to air-condition their whole house in the summer. I tried to turn the AC on in our small apartment one hot June, and our electric bill was $900 for that one month. Well, the Cap and Trade system to reduce carbon dioxide output, and subsequent environmental laws that essentially forbade using coal as a fuel source, and then mandated that one half of our electric generation come from renewable sources, drove the cost up relentlessly. Nevertheless, I guess I feel good that we are doing our part to save the planet and help the Third World to pay for clean energy.

Back to the travelogue. The four of us visited a place we had always dreamed of going – the Peoples Republic of China Yosemite Park. It still seems strange to call it that, but that is what it has been for a while. The national credit crisis of 2018, when our annual deficit first reached 3 Trillion Dollars, caused the Chinese, the Saudis and other holders of our debt to stop buying our Treasury bonds. Since two-thirds of our federal spending comes from borrowing, the Treasury Department had no choice but to entice them to continue loaning us money, and we had to offer the only collateral we owned of real value - our land. Of course, they demanded our best land – the National Parks.

Our family had been excited for months, because the Chinese government only allows 25% of the park's visitor capacity to be American citizens. We had waited four years for our turn on the list.

While we were in the vicinity, we also drove to the rim of the Saudi Arabian Grand Canyon Park. I say drive to the rim, because the Saudis prohibit anyone but Muslims from hiking down to the Colorado River and no one may raft on it. Their lawsuit to control and sell the water rights is still pending in the Supreme Court. Since two of the justices are Mullahs, the pundits from FNN (the Federal News Network) are predicting a win for the Saudis.

Seven years ago, a Supreme Court case ruled that the makeup of the Court must reflect the ethnicity and religion of the country. Muslims constitute 23% of our population, so the Court ordered that Muslims must fill the next two vacancies. That ruling also mandated Congress to embrace diversity by gradually integrating Sha'ria law into our federal statutes.

Mentioning FNN, it is really kind of funny. Twenty years ago, the acronym FNN stood for the "Fox News Network". The Broadcast Fairness and Equality Act of 2013 (which was predicated on the Fairness Doctrine of the 1980's) initiated years of lawsuits filed by MediaMatters and MoveOn.org against Fox and their parent company, News Corp. The Supreme Court ruled that the only way to ensure that the public sees completely "fair and balanced" news is for the government to manage media content. It was then a short jump to the BFE Act amendment that created the new Federal News Network.

While we were near the Grand Canyon, we also took in Las Vegas. The Saudis, who adhere to strict Islamic Wahhabi beliefs, have openly stated that they will cut off their Colorado River water to Las Vegas by next year unless it has purged itself of all sin and iniquity. Without water from Lake Meade, Las Vegas cannot survive. I am glad we were able to see Vegas now. The kids were mesmerized by the lights and fountains. The seedier aspects of the city were a little difficult to explain.

This is the first year of relaxed interstate travel restrictions, so we took full advantage of it while it lasts. Before this summer, our Federal Homeland Security Forces had restricted car travel to 50 miles and then only with a valid work-related internal visa with an official FHSF stamp. Funny, it has only been seven years since these intense security efforts started – seems so much longer. Looking back, I guess it really started in 2016, when the Obama Justice Department (after intense pressure from the ACLU and the Mexican American Legal Defense Fund) prohibited the FBI, the Border Patrol and local law enforcement agencies from "harassing" any foreigners to prevent the travesty of "racial profiling". Preceding that, the 2011 Department of Justice investigations and prosecutions had eviscerated the CIA.

It was little wonder that a gigantic wave of immigration, both legal and illegal, swept into the country. Millions of the immigrants were Muslims, fleeing the nuclear war in the Middle East. Many of these, unfortunately, were radical jihadists. In 2022, after years of planning, they launched coordinated attacks on the infidel nation that they blamed for the destruction of their homeland and the resulting exodus. By the time we became more concerned with national security than political correctness and started tracking them down, they had unleashed over 50 biological and nuclear weapons. Americans demanded a crackdown and protection, and the result, as you might imagine, was draconian. It made the Patriot Act wiretaps of 2001 and security lines at airports seem ridiculously mild in comparison. Well, I remember my Grandma saying, "an ounce of prevention is worth a pound of cure". In this case, the "pound of cure" has been tough on all of us.

As I said, the security restrictions have eased a bit, but I am not sure that it's because we are now safe, or because the 80 Muslim members of Congress have pressured the FHSF to step back.

In any event, we hit the road. Our first choice for a vacation would have been to take the children to our nation's capital, Washington D.C., to see all the Memorials, the Smithsonian, and the White House. Tragically, Washington was the target of one of the first dirty bombs, so a good portion of the District of Columbia will be radioactive beyond my lifetime. I hate that none of our family will ever get to see the original *Declaration of Independence*, but Ground Zero for the bomb was near the National Archives building and the *Declaration* was incinerated in a ball of white heat. Some journalists callously said it had been "incinerated" long before the bomb went off.

How ironic that I was born in 1984, the same year as the title of George Orwell's novel. It is sobering to see that Orwell's prediction of totalitarian government was pretty optimistic, because the United States, in this year of 2029, has eclipsed anything he could have conceived.

I am now 45 years old. In November 2006, when I was 22, I voted for a progressive Democrat Congressman that I thought best reflected my views of compassion toward the downtrodden, and was against the Iraq War. In November 2008, I voted for "Change" in the person of Barack Obama. I wanted a country free of partisan bickering, one different from my parents' stodgy Conservative views, a country united in progress. In 2010, even with the evidence of what that "Change" really was, I voted for a liberal Democrat Senator who promised to "clean up" Washington and continue to move our country towards a more fair and balanced treatment of all people. Obama got my vote for a second term in 2012, so that he could "continue the movement".

Elections, as I now know all too well, have consequences.

℘)℃ℛ

This prediction is not inevitable. The American people can shake off the manacles of complacency, break their addiction to dependency, elect principled leadership, and demand that our public officials lead this nation away from the brink of totalitarianism and back to the founding rights, freedoms, and values that made America the envy of the free world.

There are those, I know, who will say that the liberation of humanity, the freedom of man and mind, is nothing but a dream. They are right. It is the American dream.
--- Archibald MacLeish

Part One:
What Are Our Nation's Founding Rights, Principles and Values?

We hold these truths to be self-evident, that all men are created equal, that they are endowed by their Creator with certain unalienable Rights, that among these are Life, Liberty and the pursuit of Happiness. — That to secure these rights, Governments are instituted among Men, deriving their just powers from the consent of the governed....
The Declaration of Independence

Our nation was established as a bastion of freedom. This is clearly defined in our national founding document – the *Declaration of Independence*. Our founders debated over the course of several years on what freedom meant and what the relationship should be between the federal government and the people. There were experiments and iterative steps on this path. The *Articles of Confederation* governed our nation for its first   six   years.   This document, an early attempt at a constitution, proved to be too loose and chaotic. For example, under the *Articles*, the individual states could print their own currency and sign foreign treaties.

Finally, after contentious debate, study, prayer, and public input, our early leaders produced the *Constitution of the United States.* This is our national charter and clearly defines the relationship between the U.S. federal government and the citizens of the nation.

Most of the *American Rights and Principles* enumerated below are expressly stated in our founding documents. If not expressly written, they are historically evident by studying the actions and precedents of our past. These rights and principles provide the solid foundation upon which *American Values and Character* are chiseled.

I believe the following defines America -- what it stands for, what it strives for, what it should be, what it can be....

American Rights and Principles

There is a supernatural Creator who endows man with the right of liberty. This right is not bestowed by any government, it is given by God. Thus, our government is intended to recognize and preserve this God-given right, not to redefine it or modify it. Our founders openly recognized the existence of a Creator and His intention that man be subservient to God, not to a government.

Our government is intended to be a servant of the people. Our framers designed Constitutional limits on government because they feared that any institution run by men will always and ultimately tend toward increasing the power of the governors at the expense of the governed. They believed, from their experience as colonists and subjects of the British Crown, that rulers will thirst for power if unchecked. They believed that government, like fire, is a useful tool if controlled, but a dangerous destroyer if not.

Experience hath shewn, that even under the best forms of government those entrusted with power have, in time, and by slow operations, perverted it into tyranny.
---Thomas Jefferson

Our Constitution, with its subsequent amendments, was not written to define or limit individual rights, which were deemed limitless. Instead, it was intended and written to specify and strictly limit the power of the federal government. Indeed, the Ninth Amendment (of the Bill of Rights) states *"Enumeration of certain rights shall not be construed to deny or disparage others retained by the people"*. The Tenth Amendment states *"The Powers not delegated to the United States by the Constitution, nor prohibited by it to the States, are reserved to the States respectively, or to the people."* This concept could not be stated any more clearly.

All people are created equal. Every citizen is born with the same intrinsic value and rights. Historically, this has meant equality of opportunity, not equality of outcome. America is a nation forged from individuals voluntarily uniting for a common purpose. Historically, it is not a nation bound involuntarily by a collectivist manifesto. Throughout our past, Americans have rejected egalitarianism (that seeks to provide equal wealth and privileges to all people). Americans have historically recognized that true freedom means that some will have more wealth than others. This can be the result of education, hard work, special skills, opportunity, birth or just good luck. Americans have long embraced the concept that this is good, not evil or unfair, and that ultimately it provides a higher standard of living for all citizens. The American imperative has been equality of opportunity not equality of outcome.

All Americans have the freedom to prosper from their own efforts, and have the right to own property free from theft or unreasonable seizure. Americans have the right to protect their property from either one. Americans have the right to choose how best to provide for themselves and their families. Americans have the right to follow their dreams. The corollary principle is that Americans have the right to fail and to learn from failure. America is a history of success following failure.

Ralph Waldo Emerson said: *America is another name for opportunity. Our whole history appears like a last effort of divine providence on behalf of the human race.*

Americans have the right to express their views in any media and forum. These views may include criticism of the government. By historical precedent, these rights are limited only by narrow legal restrictions on slander and libel, wherein a damaging falsehood is spoken or printed about someone. There is, by legal necessity, a very high barrier to prove slander or libel occurred. There is no constitutional protection from someone being offended or having "hateful" things said about them.

Americans have the right to worship as they choose, or not to worship at all. America was founded in part to provide a home for religious people to worship as they desired. European countries of the time, particularly England, had a state religion. Some of our early colonists desired that everyone be required to participate in a mandated religious affiliation. Speaking directly to that potentiality, the First Amendment of the Constitution (the Bill of Rights) specifies that Americans have freedom from a government-mandated faith, better known as a Theocracy. This amendment further explicitly states that *"Congress shall make no law...prohibiting the free expression thereof"* (i.e. of religion). This amendment specifically intends for citizens to have the right to express their religious beliefs in any setting. Taxpayer funded settings are not excluded. This amendment clearly did not intend to deny the rights of some citizens to express their religious views so that other citizens might be spared from seeing or hearing a religious message. It was intended to allow all citizens the freedom to embrace or reject religion. Americans have freedom of religion, not freedom from religion.

Americans have the right and the obligation to vote for a representative government. In the original Constitution, the right is implied. In fact, initially, State Legislatures, not individual citizens, elected members of the U. S. Senate. Subsequent amendments and precedent have firmly established the right of citizens to vote.

American Values and Character

America was founded upon Judeo-Christian values, which have shaped the national discussion since our inception. The first peoples upon our shores included Pilgrims, Puritans and Quakers, whose beliefs were based on both the Old Testament (Hebrew scripture) and the New Testament. Their biblical inspiration for living espoused liberty, individual responsibility, education, productive work, ethical behavior and justice. The Ten Commandments formed the basis of their legal system.

Abigail Adams (wife and influential adviser to second President John Adams) wrote: *A patriot without religion in my estimation is as great a paradox as an honest Man without the fear of God. Is it possible that he whom no moral obligations bind, can have any real Good Will towards Men? Can he be a patriot who, by an openly vicious conduct, is undermining the very bonds of Society?....The Scriptures tell us "righteousness exalteth a Nation."*

There are countless such quotes from our founding fathers which invoke the guidance and protection of God in the creation of the United States. One has only to tour Washington D.C. to observe this belief engraved in marble on virtually every public building and monument.

The tip of the Washington Monument has the following inscribed: *Laus Deo*, which translates from the Latin, "Praise be to God".

The Supreme Court building, finished in 1935, has images of the Ten Commandments in multiple locations.

The Jefferson Memorial quotes: *God who gave us life gave us liberty. Can the liberties of a nation be secure when we have removed a conviction that these liberties are the gift of God? Indeed I tremble for my country when I reflect that God is just, that his justice cannot sleep forever.*

Our traditional Judeo-Christian values have influenced not only our religious beliefs but were critical in forging our work ethic, our compassion and charity, our judicial system, even our relations with other nations.

Sculpture of Moses Holding the Ten Commandments – Exterior of Supreme Court Building, Washington D.C.

Americans have an independent spirit, born initially from demanding and fighting for their freedom, and forged by conquering a continent. Historically, Americans loath, and typically will not tolerate, being dictated to.

Americans are historically self-reliant, as a nation and as individuals. Traditionally, Americans value achievement, efficiency and practicality. Throughout our past, there has been an inherent expectation that every American citizen be productive and contribute to society as best he or she can.

Try not to become a man of success but rather try to become a man of value. --- Albert Einstein

Americans have always believed that education is the foundation of self-reliance for individuals, and liberty for the nation. A skilled or educated person has the means to support him or herself and their family, and to be productive in the community. An educated and informed citizenry is more likely to understand the problems facing their nation and to be involved in the solutions.

If Virtue & Knowledge are diffused among the People, they will never be enslav'd. This will be their great Security.
--- Founding Father Samuel Adams

Americans cherish freedom of action and choice, as long as the action does not hurt or impede others.

The right to swing my fist ends where the other man's nose begins. --- Oliver Wendell Holmes, Supreme Court Justice

Americans value honesty. But we are not naïve in the belief that all people are honest. Americans expect that our system of laws and our judiciary should be intrinsically fair and unbiased, and that we have the right to hold the justice system accountable.

Americans have always included humor as an integral part of the national character and appreciate individuals who possess a good sense of humor. Humor has historically been used in our political discourse.

Humor is mankind's greatest blessing. --- Mark Twain, one of our country's most beloved authors

Americans believe in playing fair, but have always understood that life will never be fair. Americans believe that the measure of a person's character is often best demonstrated by how they deal with the low blows and failures that are an inevitable part of every life. Historically, Americans have applauded success which resulted from dogged determination to overcome failure.

Prior to our very recent past, Americans rejected perpetual victim-hood as a sustainable condition or a political tactic.

Americans are competitive and possess an innate desire to win. However, this trait is tempered by our desire for playing fair and by the rules, so it has not become an over-zealous win-at-any-cost obsession.

Americans believe that the family is the cornerstone of American society. That parents have the responsibility to nurture, provide for and raise their children. Americans believe that the nuclear family is the most critical source for teaching (and demonstrating) values to children.

The group consisting of mother, father and child is the main educational agency of mankind.
--- Dr. Martin Luther King, Jr.

Americans believe they have a responsibility as individuals to support a community. The community may include neighbors, churches, civic organizations, youth groups and schools. The American way is to volunteer time and effort to enhance the community where we live. Americans firmly believe that volunteerism is a responsibility and a privilege of citizenship.

Americans believe in charity and compassion. Americans believe in voluntarily giving of their time and treasure to help others, through both religious and secular venues. Americans historically have responded to those in need, without being coerced or forced. In fact, Americans traditionally dislike being coerced or forced in any fashion.

America is great because she is good. If America ceases to be good, America will cease to be great.
--- Alexis de Tocqueville

Americans are action-oriented and believe that we can control and shape our future. We reject the fatalism found in other cultures that accepts the present as an historical inevitability and views the future as being in the hands of fate. Our Judeo-Christian heritage has taught us that God offers us a Free Will.

President Ronald Reagan left us this belief:
Standing on the tiny deck of the Arabella in 1630, off the Massachusetts coast, John Winthrop said: "We will be as a city upon a hill. The eyes of all people are upon us..."

We cannot escape our destiny, nor should we try to do so. The leadership of the free world was thrust upon us two centuries ago in that little hall in Philadelphia.

In the days following World War II, when the economic strength and power of America was all that stood between the world and a return to the dark ages, Pope Pius XII said: "The American people have a great genius for splendid and unselfish actions. Into the hands of America God has placed the destinies of an afflicted mankind."

We are indeed, and we are today, the last best hope of man on earth.

Part Two:
How American Rights, Principles and Values Have Been Attacked and Subverted for the Past Seventy-five Years -- The Ascendency of Neo-totalitarianism.

All tyranny needs to gain a foothold is for people of good conscience to remain silent. ---Thomas Jefferson

The following discussions address what I believe are the past actions and the current issues that most imperil our American way of life. It is not intended to be exhaustive, and the reader may feel there are other events or scenarios that have had more detrimental impact. What is beyond question, as will be shown, is that if we as a country do not alter course, our grandchildren will not recognize the United States of America as we have known it.

The New Deal

A discussion of the decline in American values must begin with Franklin Roosevelt's New Deal in the 1930's. Other Conservative political thinkers trace the decline to Theodore Roosevelt, Woodrow Wilson, and the Progressive Movement that flourished in the early decades of the 20th century. In fact, there were two events resulting from this movement that ultimately had great impact on the future growth of federal power.

The first of these two events was the 16th Amendment, passed in 1913, that authorized the federal government to collect taxes on an individual's income. This dramatically increased the ability of the federal government to fund its expansion of power. One might wonder why citizens of the U.S. would accept such a tax. The answer is that passage of the tax was promoted as a way to make "rich" people pay the nation's tab. The average citizen was led to believe they would never be subject to it. In 1913, less than 1% of the population paid any income tax. Even in 1918, after several income tax hikes, and the need to fund our involvement in World War I, only 5% of the population paid the tax.[4]

The second significant event of the Progressive Era was the 17th Amendment, also passed in 1913, that required U.S. Senators to be selected by direct elections of the citizens. Prior to the amendment, they were elected by each state legislature. The reason for this, as explained in the *Federalist Papers*, was to achieve true decentralized bicameralism, and to effectively diffuse legislative power.

In republican government, the legislative authority, necessarily predominate. The remedy for this inconveniency is, to divide the legislature into different branches; and to render them by different modes of election, and different principles of action, as little connected with each other, as the nature of their common functions and their common dependencies on the society, will admit.
--- James Madison, Federalist No 51

Passage of the 17th Amendment was sold as a means to increase democracy and eliminate bribery and corruption in state bodies. It also avoided deadlocks in state legislatures which had often resulted in Senate vacancies. The ultimate impact was to effectively remove from federal representation the states themselves. No one was involved in decision making at the federal level who had as their primary goal the active representation of the states. It made state governments simply an administrative arm of the expanding federal bureaucracy.

In many respects, the early Progressive's influence was primarily rhetorical. Governmental intervention during this time was often specifically targeted, and did not have the widespread influence on values that ultimately transpired during the New Deal. The 16th and 17th Amendments had little effect until wielded by the New Dealers. The early Progressives may have planted the seeds of destruction, but the New Deal actually bore the fruit.

In 1932, after three years of economic depression, increased bank failures, and escalating unemployment, Franklin D. Roosevelt became President. The American electorate had lost patience with Herbert Hoover. His administration's interventionist programs and policies had been unsuccessful in lifting the nation out of the Great

Depression. Taking full advantage of his Congressional Democrat majority, and the mandate they believed they had been given, FDR and his "Brain Trust" unleashed a plethora of collectivist programs and federal spending to combat the Depression. Strongly influenced by British economist John Maynard Keynes[5], the Administration believed in massive federal spending (which of course resulted in massive increased taxation and/or debt) to kick start the economy and provide relief to a citizenry in despair.

From 1933 to 1940, the federal budget more than doubled, growing from $4.6 billion to $9.5 billion. Each year, about one half the spending came from borrowed funds.[6] Money poured into numerous federal employment and relief programs (such as the Federal Emergency Relief Administration, Works Progress Administration, Public Works Administration, Civilian Conservation Corps, Tennessee Valley Authority, and National Housing Act), into farm subsidies (the Agricultural Adjustment Act), into old age pensions (the Social Security Act), into rural electrification (the Rural Electrification Act), and into other bureaucracies.

In 1933, the National Industrial Recovery Act was passed, which suspended the Sherman Antitrust Act and permitted trade and industrial associations to seek the Administration's approval to form "codes of fair competition", essentially allowing collusion and cartels. FDR hoped that this would result in efficient centralized planning of industrial output, reduced competition, increased production and, hopefully, increased employment. The Act also guaranteed union bargaining rights, and regulated working standards (work hours, pay levels, etc.) In 1935, the Supreme Court ruled much of the Act unconstitutional.

For two years, the NIRA tremendously increased governmental bureaucracy and oversight. The National Recovery Administration approved 557 basic and 189 supplemental industry codes, produced about 3,000 administrative orders running to over 10,000 pages, and offered thousands of opinions and guides from national, regional, and local code boards, which interpreted and enforced the Act. Implementation was so ponderous that it proved ineffective in achieving desired improvements.[7] What it did successfully was introduce the idea that heavy governmental regulation of business was necessary and acceptable.

The National Labor Relations Act (which was intended to continue the provisions of the NIRA) vastly increased the collective bargaining power of unions, spawning the golden age of union membership, negotiated wage increases and employment benefits. Union bargaining units initially won many of the benefits that employees take for granted today. Only in later years, were working hours, safety conditions, minimum wages, etc. mandated by the federal government. Empowering labor unions, however, did not encourage businesses to hire more employees; it actually did more to continue high unemployment than to create jobs.[8]

Consider the following analysis of the motives of the New Dealers. It was written by a respected political journalist of the era, Walter Lippman, and appeared in the New York Herald Tribune in May 1939:

Between the [factions within] the New Dealers, the crucial difference is, I think, that the one group is interested primarily in social reform and the other is interested primarily in control of the economic system. Among the Radical New Dealers, the essence of the New Deal is the reduction of private corporate control by collective bargaining and labor legislation on the one side, and by restrictive, competitive and deterrent government action on the other side. The Reformers wish to spend, one because they wish to create social services and public works; two because they wish to prime the pump for recovery. The Radicals wish to spend, one because public spending increases the power of the government as compared with private business; two because it makes recovery and prosperity depend on government rather than private initiative. The Reformers regard the spending as an instrument of recovery and a means for improving the condition of the people. The Radicals regard the spending as a substitute for recovery and as a means of altering the balance of social power.[9]

The New Deal undoubtedly provided government paychecks and thus short-term relief for many American citizens. Many of the financial regulatory reforms instituted during this time were beneficial and remain to this day. Among them the Federal Deposit Insurance Corporation and the Securities and Exchange Commission.

Yet, the New Deal did not end the Depression. For the most part, new governmental intervention began to wane after 1937, although the previous spending programs continued. By 1939, GDP had grown, but was largely driven by federal spending, not true economic revival. Unemployment had decreased, but was still unacceptably high at 17%. Most economic historians agree that the awakening of the American industrial giant prior to and during World War II, was the real reason the Depression ended.[10]

So we see that governmental intervention, by Hoover Republicans and Roosevelt Democrats, exacerbated a moderate recession (which is a natural and unavoidable factor in free market cycles) into a deeper economic depression, and then prolonged the crisis and made it far worse. The private sector was so regulated, manipulated and taxed, that it became afraid to spend, expand and hire.

Amity Shales, in her work *The Forgotten Man,* concludes: *"But the deepest problem was the intervention, the lack of faith in the marketplace. Government management of the late 1920's and 1930's hurt the economy. Both Hoover and Roosevelt misstepped in a number of ways. Such forays prevented recovery and took the country into the depression within the Depression of 1937 and 1938."* [11]

On the other hand, there are theorists who maintain that New Deal Keynesian theory was correct, but that the government's intervention was too timid and limited. They contend massive fiscal intervention (supposedly more massive than doubling the federal budget) would have righted our economic ship more quickly. Robert McElvane, in his book *The Great Depression,* claimed, *"There is little doubt that a full-scale Keynesian program could have ended the Depression."* [12] However, this philosophy is inconsistent with prudent economic theory and has been contradicted by economic history.

As demonstrated during the recessions of 1981-1982 and 2000-2001, reducing taxes and thus increasing dollars in private hands does far more to truly stimulate economic growth than throwing federal money at politically selected targets.

Today, the incredible fiscal policy spending of the Obama Administration, and his Democrat majority in Congress, has failed to generate a sustained recovery in employment or housing, and, as of this writing, the fear generated by deficit spending and our looming National Debt has the country on the brink of a "double dip" recession, if not an outright depression. (When plotting Gross Domestic Product (GDP) against time, a W-shaped curve, called "double dip" recession, occurs when the economy slides into recession, emerges from the recession with a short burst of growth, but quickly falls back into recession.)

What is indisputable is that the New Deal radically changed the relationship between the government and the governed. As such, it began a gradual deterioration of the values that had defined America since its founding.

The New Deal, by creating government relief and work programs, encouraged our population to become dependent on government. The New Deal was the birth of the welfare state in America. Moreover, through incessant government propaganda, from visual icons to fireside chats, our people were made to feel that these emergency programs were the norm, that they were acceptable government services, and should even be considered a "right".

Indeed, in his 1944 State of the Union speech, Roosevelt proposed a "Second Bill of Rights" which redefined rights not in terms of freedoms but in terms of economic security (e.g. a home, a job, medical care, education)[13]. A later section of this book will explore in more detail the current state of dependency in our country -- today's harvest, sowed by the seeds of the New Deal.

The New Deal first generated the widespread expectation in the media and the electorate that government is the first and best solver of problems (even though it did not solve the immediate problem). It created the beginnings of a belief system in which the American people and American businesses are absolved of all responsibility because the paternalistic government is the ultimate protector and defender.

The New Deal unleashed federal intervention into the U.S. private enterprise system.   Certainly, there had been intervention prior to the Depression, for example, anti-trust and food and drug manufacturing safety legislation. But those efforts were meek in comparison to the rules, restrictions, tariffs, taxes, programs, and controls imposed upon American businesses in the 1930's.   Thus, the New Deal made the federal government a full partner in the conduct of American business, established its behavior as a legitimate precedent, and created the expectation that government was capable of successfully mitigating the natural imbalances, and subsequent re-balancing, that occur in free markets. Our citizens now had the belief that government must control economic cycles.

The New Deal also redefined the relationship between employer and employee. In some ways, this was good and redressed abuses that had existed.   The longer term consequences, however, significantly shifted the balance of power in favor of labor unions, and emboldened collectivist thought and expectations among our workforce. New Deal governmental / labor activism laid the foundation for increasingly over-generous collective bargaining agreements, which have ultimately damaged our economic competitiveness and resulted in painful economic corrections.   These corrections have been rippling through American private enterprise for years. The airline and automotive industries are but recent examples.

Units of American government at all levels, which have empowered labor unions only within the last twenty five years, are just beginning to deal with the hard choices of providing the generous wages, benefits and pensions that were negotiated by politicians now long gone, versus the increased taxation that will be required to provide them.

The New Deal eroded individualism of thought and action that had been the hallmark of American character. In Hayek's *The Road to Serfdom,* one is left with the overall feeling that the "unity of purpose" exhibited during extreme times, such as depression or war, is really quite atypical; that in normal times, people have a far greater, indeed an infinite, variety of non-forced choices that influence behavior.[14] It takes little effort of the imagination to recognize what this elevated level of government control, during this unique period in our history, would mean for the exercise of individual thought and liberty.

New Deal programs intensified the division of the American people into class-oriented "interest groups", each with its own political agenda. The Roosevelt Administration forged a coalition of labor unions, relief recipients, Blacks, the elderly, Southern Democrats, religious minorities, intellectuals and farmers. They then catered to each with targeted regulation, spending programs and rhetoric.[15] Thus, the New Deal began the transformation of an America that had traditionally prided itself on being free from a rigid, hereditary class structure into a nation of "protected" classes. Each protected class ultimately must be courted by its respective protecting politicians, and rewarded with redistributed governmental largesse. Of course, by definition, the classes must be protected *from* someone or something. Therefore they must be pitted against one another or against other villains (such as the evil rich or greedy businesses) in continuous class warfare. This is a flawed and destructive political posture and is inconsistent with addressing our national issues.

The New Deal created the first nation-wide, universal welfare program -- Social Security. Begun as a supplement to aid the elderly and provide a decent life in their waning years, it unfortunately was founded as a financial "Ponzi" scheme, wherein the current beneficiaries are paid their pensions not from any savings or contributions that they themselves made, but from taxes remitted by current workers. Thus, those who have been taxed to provide current benefits feel (justifiably so) that they are entitled to receive their Social Security benefits when they retire, even though no retirement account assets exist to provide those benefits. The age of entitlement mentality had begun in America.

The New Deal started our country on the slippery slope to egalitarianism, that is, the belief that our citizens deserve equality in income and possessions. And that if they do not achieve their rightful income or possessions, it is not their fault. Others (greedy corporations, Big Oil, Wall Street, the "Rich", the "Man") have stymied them. Roosevelt, in his 1944 State of the Union address, said that our *"political rights have proved inadequate to assure us equality in the pursuit of happiness"*[16]. Stated in another way, the New Deal subtly began the acceptance of the maxim *From each according to his ability, to each according to his need.* The quote, of course, is from Karl Marx, co-author of *The Communist Manifesto.*

The New Deal was the beginning of a societal sea-change that continues to this day. The American people began trading liberty for security.

Those who would give up essential Liberty, to purchase a little temporary Safety, deserve neither Liberty nor Safety.
--- Benjamin Franklin

Escalating Use of Debt to Fund Government Spending

The federal budget for 2010 required that almost one half of all federal spending comes from borrowed money.[17] This is astounding and reckless! Our political leaders from both parties have ignored the most basic of financial principles....to live within your means. American families at all income levels know this very simple truth. Living beyond your ability to pay for your lifestyle will lead to financial ruin.

Debt is not necessarily destructive. A family can incur a mortgage to buy a home, and so long as they can afford the mortgage payments (i.e. the debt service), the mortgage debt is beneficial, not harmful. However, when the family buys more house than they can afford, the debt service becomes far too large a percentage of their income, they find it difficult to afford the interest payments, and financial difficulty ensues. It is not dissimilar for our federal government.

Our nation has used debt to fund operations since its inception. Our revolutionary forefathers borrowed money from foreign governments to pay for our battle for freedom. Government can effectively use debt to fund extraordinary situations or cover emergency shortfalls. The United States has incurred debt throughout its history, but until the 1930's, the national debt was primarily the result of financing wars.[18]

However, our nation is now succumbing to a philosophy espoused by Keynesian economists for decades that larger and larger amounts of federal debt are acceptable so long as it falls below some arbitrary percentage of Gross Domestic Product (i.e. the total value of the goods and services produced by the U.S. economy). This philosophy theorizes that our economy can somehow overcome massive federal debt through economic expansion and inflation.[19]

Those who believe in this philosophy accept this ever-expanding debt as a permanent fixture of our federal government and do not ever intend to enact balanced annual budgets, much less pay back the outstanding debt. By accepting this economic fantasy, our leaders are gambling with our nation's future, and risking the opportunities and standard of living for our posterity. It is a direct rebuttal of the ideals expressed in the Declaration of Independence.

Like so many of the problems we have seen unfold in the last few years, the use of massive debt began during the Roosevelt New Deal, ostensibly to pull the country out of economic depression. Roosevelt's Democrat Administration began profligate spending of money the government did not have. Political *spinmeisters* euphemistically call this "fiscal policy".

During and immediately after World War II, our national debt escalated to over 100% of GDP (peaking at 113%)[20]. This was due to the annual deficits incurred by New Deal fiscal spending, followed by the costs of fighting the largest war ever witnessed on our planet. During this war, which we fought on two global fronts, we not only fielded and supplied an enormous American force, but also used our industrial might to equip our British Commonwealth and

Soviet allies. Moreover, after the end of the war, our country pumped millions of dollars into post-war Europe via the Marshall plan, and to a lesser extent, post-war Japan.

As this war effort wound down, our leaders recognized that our debt level was not sustainable, and through spending restraint, balanced budgets, and remarkable economic expansion, the national debt was incrementally reduced as a percentage of GDP. We actually maintained annual federal budget surpluses in 1947, '48, '51, '56, '57, and '60.[21] Our leaders and our citizens of that generation viewed the debt as a one-time emergency and not a perpetual financial albatross. This generation has lately retained the sobriquet of "The Greatest Generation". Of all their accomplishments, their financial maturity, self-reliance and self-sacrifice for future generations may be what truly made them "great".

However, it appears that the deficit spending genie, once let out of the bottle, has been uncontrollable. In the eighty years since 1930, we have had a balanced federal budget in only *nine* of those years[22]. It is far too easy for politicians to buy popularity and votes by spending now, and then turn their backs and refuse to consider how, or by whom, it is to be repaid. The people of this country have been systematically fleeced by an irresponsible political class intent on furthering a monumental fiscal atrocity for simple expediency. Outrageous, but as maddening as this is.....we are all to blame.

The first graph below, based on Congressional Budget Office (CBO) data, is a dramatic visual illustration of how our annual federal spending has exceeded revenues in almost every year in our recent history[23]. That is, our federal government ran a *deficit* in each of those years.

These annual deficits contribute to an ever-growing national debt (i.e. the total amount we owe). The second graph uses CBO data to project this frightening trend into the future. Note that the CBO analysis explains that their projections actually understate the debt because it assumes that interest rates remain stable, rather than increase, as a reaction to the inevitable pressure of increased debt levels.

To interpret these graphs, the lightly shaded portion of each bar is the revenue our government collected, or is projected to collect each year (including FICA taxes). The total height of each bar indicates the amount of money that the federal government has spent or projects to spend. (including Social Security, Medicare/Medicaid, and Other Spending). The difference, depicted as the dark portion of each bar, is our actual or projected annual deficit in each year.

As a result of these annual deficits, in the last forty years, our *Debt Held By The Public* has grown from $283 Billion to $8.6 Trillion (in nominal dollars) -- a 2,936% increase[24]. The last ten years have been the budgetary equivalent of *Alice in Wonderland*. The Bush Administration lowered taxes but increased spending dramatically on war-making and new entitlements. The Obama Administration and his Democrat Congress have taken spending money we do not have to absolutely absurd and irresponsible levels. Warren Buffett has reportedly said: *"Fiscally, we are in uncharted territory".*

What would happen to a family, or a business, acting in this same manner? In the Summer of 2010, our national *Debt Held By The Public* was $8.6 Trillion or 58% of Projected 2010 GDP[25].

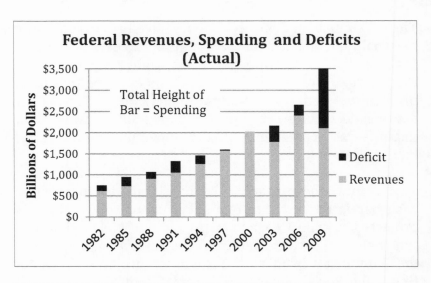

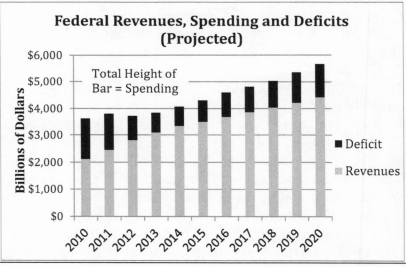

At this moment, we owe over one half of what we produce. Annual deficits are projected to be between $724 Billion and $1.5 Trillion over the next ten years (at the *current* rate of spending, not including the impact of Obamacare). The Congressional Budget Office is projecting our debt will be 87% of GDP by 2020, and 101% by 2023[26]. In thirteen *short* years, our debt will exceed what our economy produces. It will strangle us.

The national debt juggernaut is disastrously out of control. The consequences will be staggering. The graph on this page depicts this stunningly dangerous prediction. Note that the CBO has determined that the *Alternative Fiscal Scenario* is the "more realistic picture of the nation's underlying fiscal policy".[27] As our debt consumes exponentially more of our Gross Domestic Product, our economic vitality will be smothered.

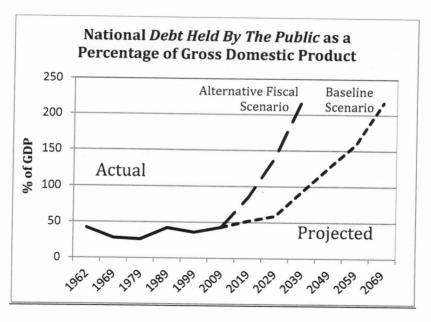

Prominent economists Reinhart and Rogoff have written a compelling book titled *This Time is Different - Eight Centuries of Financial Folly*, in which they describe research that spans 800 years and examines national economies, emerging and established, medieval to modern. They consistently find that excessive debt (typically past 90% of GDP) is a tipping point in economic growth.

Beyond that tipping point, nations cannot grow their way out of debt. They are faced with the painful consequences of draconian spending cuts, savings and repayment, high inflation, or the even more painful option of default.[28]

So far, we have only quoted the official *Debt Held By The Public*, which are the notes, bonds, TIPS, etc., held by parties external to the U.S. government. Interest must actually be paid on this debt. The $8.6 Trillion does not include the *Intergovernmental Holding Debt*, currently at $4.5 Trillion, which is primarily the I.O.U.s that the federal government owes the Social Security and Medicare Trust Funds. Adding these debts together comprises the *Total Public Debt*, which as of this writing is $13,000,000,000,000[29].

Thirteen Trillion Dollars. Most Americans have no concept of what that amount of money really is. Here is a helpful visualization. If you had started spending One Million Dollars on the day Jesus was born over two thousand years ago, and spent One Million Dollars every single day since, as of today you still would not have spent a trillion dollars. If we allocate that debt to every person in America, it means that a baby born today owes over $42,000 before he or she takes their first breath.

If the *Total Public Debt* were not horrendous enough, it does not include the current projections for Social Security and Medicare benefits promised to future generations that exceed projected future contributions. The amount of these unfunded entitlements approximate $106.8 Trillion (Medicare is 84% of that amount).[30] Let that statistic sink in for just a moment. If a private pension fund or insurance company operated in this fashion, the administrators would be convicted of criminal mismanagement and would join Bernard Madoff in federal prison.

Our nation now spends 6% of our budget simply to pay the interest on the Debt Held By The Public. The Congressional Budget Office projects that in ten years, our debt service will consume 14% of our budget[31]. In twenty years, our debt service will be the single largest expenditure in the federal budget, exceeding even Social Security.[32] This is a national death spiral. As we pay more in interest each year, our annual deficit becomes larger, our total debt is thus increased and we must pay even more interest in future years.

The truly frightening aspect of this scenario is that the projection of 14% is based on current, historically low interest rates. Almost every economist projects that interest rates will rise, and accordingly, the amount of interest we must pay back increases. What will we do when interest rates rise to historically normal levels? What in heaven's name will we do if interest rates rise to the 20% level we saw in the early 1980's? Our political class is literally rolling the dice with our nation's future, and the odds are stacked against us.

We are committing national financial suicide. In truth, a more apt description of our current financial policies is national child abuse. We are killing our children's financial future. We are committing generational theft. We should be ashamed. We should remember the words of our forefather, Thomas Paine, whose work helped inspire our fight for freedom: *If there must be trouble, let it be in my day, that my child may have peace.*

Moreover, almost half of our debt is held by foreign nations, including China, Japan, and Saudi Arabia[33]. We are transferring massive amounts of wealth from the United States to other countries. We are risking a massive transfer of power from us to them. Will they be as generous and merciful to our country as we have been to the world? This is unlikely.

Perhaps the most damaging result of our reliance on deficit spending is the impact it has had on our national psyche. Our citizens, having seen the financial irresponsibility of our federal government, have accepted deficit spending as a way of life personally. For twenty years, we have used credit cards to buy now and pay later, or declare bankruptcy and not pay at all. For twenty years, American families purchased larger and larger homes that they could not really afford but that ridiculous lending standards allowed (until that bubble burst in 2007). For twenty years, our individual savings rate has dwindled, and in many years was negative. According to a May 2010 survey by Experian, the *average* per capita consumer debt in the U.S. was almost $25,000[34].

Our government's profligate ways have mutilated traditional American values of fiscal prudence and self-responsibility.

Unreasonable "Progressive" Taxation

It is time for those riding in the wagon to get out and help the rest of us pull the wagon.--- Senator Phil Gramm

In the first place, the term "progressive" is a horrendous misnomer. It is progressive only in the sense that it is progressively unfair. Our tax system increases the amount of money that must be paid as incomes rise. Our tax code also increases the *percentage* of income that must be paid as the level of income rises.

Tax statistics are boring. Their dryness, however, does not in the least diminish how frightening they are when viewed in terms of their societal impact. The table below depicts the impact of our "progressive" federal income tax system. The data in the table is for the tax year ending 2007, and updated in July 2009[35].

Percentile of US Households	Household Income($)	% of All 2007 Taxes Paid By the Households	% of Total 2007 AGI* Earned by Households	% of All 1987 Taxes Paid By the Households
Lower 50%	<32,879	3%	12.2%	6%
Upper 50%	>32,879	97%	87.7%	94%
Upper 10%	>113,018	71%	48.0%	56%
Upper 5%	>160,041	61%	37.4%	43%
Upper 1%	>410,096	40%	22.8%	NA

* Adjusted Gross Income

In 2007, fifty percent of the households in this country earned 12% of the income but only paid 3% of the taxes. Ten percent of our households earned 48% of the income but paid 71% of the taxes. This tax burden distribution is not "progressive", it is grossly unfair, and, as discussed below, it is destructive. Please note that this analysis *does not include* the increased taxation that will result from the Obama Administration and the current Democrat-led Congress.

When the statistics from 2007 are compared to 1987, it is clear that the tax-burden-shift is becoming ever more onerous for Americans who attempt to increase their earning power and thus their standard of living. This is not coincidental, and is the policy of our federal government, whether Republicans or Democrats are in power. Also, please note that this time period includes the Bush tax reductions of 2001, which, according to political rhetoric, were only to benefit the "wealthy". If that was their intent, they failed. In reality, the tax reductions of 2001 benefited all taxpayers, and *increased* the number of people who pay no income tax (or even receive tax credit payments), thus enlarging the portion of all taxes that must be paid by higher earners.

Moreover, when consideration is given to how these tax dollars are distributed via governmental largesse, the inequality becomes even more alarming. The Tax Foundation prepares an in-depth analysis of taxpayers versus tax-consumers.[36] This study separated American households into groups based on income earned, and then calculated for each group the per household amount of federal spending from which they benefited. The estimate of federal benefit dollars received is a per capita allocation of federal outlays based on the numbers of citizens eligible to receive them. For example, all citizens benefit from defense spending, highway spending, etc., whereas seniors are the primary beneficiaries from Medicare spending and low income citizens benefit from Medicaid or Title I education spending.

The chart below, which is based on 2010 estimates, graphically depicts this disparity. The twelve Family Income Groups along the bottom axis represent the family incomes that fall within each percentage. For example, the "0-10%" group represents the 10% of American families that make the lowest incomes. The "50-60%" group represents the ten percent of American families that fall within that income level. The "99-100%" represents the 1% of families that make the highest incomes. The left axis represents the number of dollars of federal spending that benefited a family per each dollar of taxes they paid.

So, for example, the lowest income group (the "0-10%" group) received $10.44 in federal spending for each dollar of taxes they paid. The highest income families received 43 cents in federal spending for each dollar of taxes they paid.

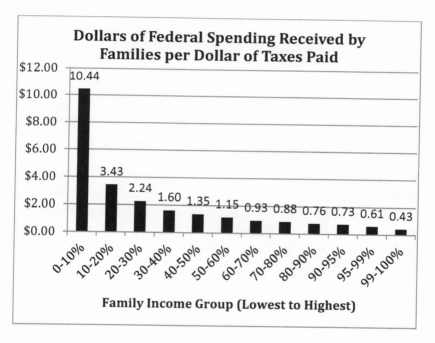

The inequalities of our progressive tax system do not end there. *For tax year 2009, 47% of tax filers paid no income tax.* (As a stark comparison of this trend, in 1969, only 16% of filers paid no tax.[37]) Additionally, 40% of tax filers not only paid zero tax, they received a government check, either through the Earned Income Tax Credit or the Child Tax Credit[38]. In 2008, these welfare payments disguised as tax credits totaled $70 Billion[39]. When one-half of the people in our country do not pay income taxes, they have no motivation or desire for governmental efficiency or restraint. In fact, human nature dictates that they will demand (and vote for) more government spending simply because they do not have to pay the tab.

As I've heard Senator Phil Gramm say: *As soon as you get more people in the wagon than pullin' the wagon, the wagon stops.* Clearly, our current tax system is creating dependency and penalizing self-responsibility. It rewards reliance on the paternalistic Nanny State, while punishing those who seek to improve their standard of living by earning higher incomes. *Common sense screams at us that this is a destructive path for our nation!*

Despite these facts, the current Administration feels that "the rich" are still not paying their fair share. Congressional Democrats believe that massive additional federal spending must be accomplished by levying more taxes on those that already pay almost all the taxes. As evidence, consider the 2010 Health Reform Act which levies enormous new taxes on families making over $250,000, to pay for coverage for the uninsured.

This is an effective class warfare tactic, but disastrous economic policy.

When the annual deficits predicted by the Congressional Budget Office become reality, and our national debt escalates as described in the previous section, it is highly unlikely that proposed tax increases will be limited to "the rich". After a highly touted effort at "middle class" tax cuts proves unsustainable, tax increases will strike the entire spectrum of tax-paying households.

One forecast, by a former Comptroller General of the United States, is that federal taxes will have to *double* within the next 20 to 30 years[40].   Every household's disposable income will diminish to fund stimulus spending, new social programs and interest payments. Less disposable income translates directly into a lowered standard of living for all working American families, and less freedom to pursue their dreams. Every dollar sent to the government is one dollar less of freedom for you.

Pundits have sarcastically termed this impact as "trickle up poverty".

(And, of course, we are only speaking of federal income taxes. This discussion has not even touched upon the increases in Social Security and Medicare/Medicaid taxes that are inevitable to make these programs financially sound again, nor the planned or proposed increases in federal estate taxes, gas taxes, capital gains taxes, carbon taxes, taxes on employer health insurance benefits, Value Added Taxes, etc. In 2009, the federal cigarette tax was increased by over 100% to fund an increase in the State Children's Health Insurance Program.)

Inevitably, as our "progressive" tax system continues to penalize earners, the dependent class will grow, putting even more strain on social programs, demanding more spending and more taxes. However, there will be fewer earners and lower incomes from which to take the taxes. The spiral of decline will be grim.

The problem with socialism is that you eventually run out of other peoples' money. --- Margaret Thatcher

Our government's tax policy is deliberately de-incentivizing the work ethic of American capitalism. Historically, our people have known that they had the freedom to prosper from their labors and freedom from unreasonable confiscation of their property. Our progressive tax code is destroying these freedoms. It is very likely this will cause a structural change in our society. American ingenuity will invent ways to shelter income and avoid taxes instead of increasing business production and creating self-sustaining jobs. Tax cheating (and associated costs of enforcement) will increase. High-income earners may simply leave and take their wealth with them. Small business entrepreneurs (the foundation of our economy) may be threatened. Logically, why become educated, or take risks, or work hard to earn more, when you will not reap the rewards?

The U.S. economy could increasingly go "underground" to avoid massive taxation. A recent Fox News analysis estimated that 7% of our Gross Domestic Product (GDP) takes place in untaxed transactions between individuals. Our more heavily taxed European cousins have a much higher percentage of untaxed transactions; for example, Greece's underground economy is 25% of its GDP, Italy's is 22%, and Spain and Portugal's are 19%[41]. The lost tax revenue from these transactions must be recovered either by higher taxes on honest citizens, or by borrowing more dollars.

Moreover, onerous and burdensome taxation attacks the charity and compassion that are traditional American values. As government confiscates and consumes more and more of our disposable income, and uses it to provide a plethora of welfare and entitlement programs, individuals can no longer afford to donate to charitable causes, nor feel there is a need, since the paternalistic government has taken on the responsibility.

"No Taxation Without Representation". Simply put, were it not for the revolutionaries who took this stand almost

240 years ago, we would not have the privileges, rights, wealth, and security we now enjoy as citizens of the United States. This slogan meant that those who were paying taxes to their country also had the *right* to govern that country. America exists only because a small number of people felt strongly about unfair taxation and subsequently took severe risks to correct it.

We are almost certainly approaching a similar tipping point.

The Addictive Power of Entitlements

There are, of course, the Big Three: Social Security, Medicare and Medicaid. These provide retirement payments, disability payments, medical care and long-term nursing home care to millions of American citizens. At this moment, they are the single largest source of federal expenditures[42]. Projected federal spending on the Big Three entitlement programs is the single most intractable problem we face in controlling deficits, and preventing a debt-fueled financial disaster in our national future.

Setting aside for a moment the current national threat from their fiscal unsustainability, these national welfare programs (for that is exactly what they are) have turned us into a nation of supplicants. We have become locked in the addictive embrace of entitlement programs.

As previously discussed, Franklin Roosevelt's New Deal created the Social Security system. Lyndon Johnson and the Democrat-led congress of the mid-1960's enacted more massive national entitlement "Ponzi" schemes -- Medicare and Medicaid -- which have vastly exceeded any cost projection made when created, are marked by waste and fraud, and are rapidly careening towards insolvency. George W. Bush, and a Republican Congress abandoned fiscal conservatism and added the Medicare Part D Prescription Drug benefit into the mix.

Human nature will not be over-ruled or denied, nor can we suspend the laws of economics. A population that has been deceived into thinking they were paying into an "old age pension program" (and a retirement health insurance program) and that receives regular documentation detailing the money they have paid into this "system" and the benefits they have been promised, is essentially hooked. No matter that they were really paying a tax; no matter that there are no actual individual accounts, no assets, no plan investments, nor any of the normal requirements for a pension fund to survive.[43] We, as a nation, have become addicted to a false promise.

This is the insidious nature of our old age entitlement programs. Most of our citizens do not feel like they are "freeloaders". We have paid into these programs during our entire working lives, and when our turn comes, we darn sure deserve "our" money. What's fair is fair. Unfortunately, there is no "our" money.

Fairness has nothing to do with government entitlements. The government made the rules; they can change the rules, and we are along for the ride. This leads to the real tragedy of the Social Security and Medicare entitlements. Theoretically, there are Trust Funds for Social Security and Medicare. This "pot" of money should contain all of the surplus FICA and Medicare contributions made by Americans in the years when there were many more contributors than retirees, especially after taxes were raised in 1983 to stabilize the system for the "foreseeable future". If this were a private system, these surpluses would have been invested conservatively, and would have grown sufficiently to cover future retirees.

That treasure chest of unused "surplus" public money was just too tempting to our political class. Sadly, surplus cash placed in the Trust Funds has been used to purchase non-negotiable government bonds, backed not by real assets, but by "the full faith and credit of the U.S. Government". In other words, the government borrowed the surplus. (In the previous section discussing our national debt, this was identified as the Intergovernmental Holding Debt.) Beginning with the 1968 Unified Federal Budget concept, all federal receipts and outflows were merged. There are no longer factual Social Security or Medicare Trust Funds, there are only IOU's.[44]

The raid on Trust Funds, while disgusting, is not the worst problem we face concerning federal entitlements. Our national demographics are a ticking financial bomb. The enormous Baby Boomer generation is just entering their retirement years. According to the 2009 Social Security and Medicare Trustees Reports, the amount by which future payouts exceed projected contributions for federal entitlement commitments, is $106.8 Trillion.[45]   This obligation is not even included in our official national debt. It is "off the balance sheet", Enron-style accounting. Yet our leaders have taken no action to avoid the pending financial disaster.

Not only are the old age entitlement programs addictive to our entire population, there are many welfare programs which entrap subsets of our people just as surely as a cook-spoon full of crack cocaine. Great Society programs such as Medicaid, Temporary Assistance to Needy Families (TANF), Food Stamps, school breakfast and lunch programs, public housing, Section 8 Housing Vouchers,

Head Start, Supplemental Security Income, State Children's Health Insurance Program, etc. however well-intentioned they might have been, have created generations of welfare-addicted recipients/victims.[46] Millions of children have grown up in households that are partially or completely supported by welfare programs. They know no other life. They have no role models for self-sufficiency and independence. They very naturally come to believe and expect that they do not need to earn their livelihood and support themselves. They are addicted to the Nanny State.

These welfare programs have spawned the academic specialty of Social Services and an entire "industry" devoted to using tax dollars (and charitable contributions) to provide a vast range of money and services to the needy. An argument can be made that this nationwide corps of publically and privately funded social workers is an enabler of the addiction of our population to entitlements and welfare.

Just as entitlements are addictive on the receiving end, apparently our political class becomes addicted to providing them. They just cannot seem to restrain themselves. The following anecdote would be ironic and humorous, if it were not so tragic. On April 14, 2010, Federal Reserve Chairman Ben Bernanke testified before the Joint Economic Committee of Congress, stating that *"Policy makers must move decisively toward sustainable fiscal balance"*, and that *"Postponing will only make it more difficult"*, and that we as a nation face *"difficult choices"*[47]

On that very same day, April 14th, Senate Democrats forced a vote which approved $18 Billion in deficit spending to extend jobless benefits[48]. In addition, a Democrat senator proposed a $23 Billion debt-funded bailout, so that public schools could avoid layoffs (which the Obama

Administration immediately endorsed)[49], and HHS Secretary Sebelius announced that her department would develop a national program (which of course translates to more deficit spending) to reduce health care "disparities"[50].

Addictive substances, whether they are government entitlement programs or opiate drugs, have two things in common. When first administered, they feel good to the person receiving them. They may offer a temporary benefit or they may create a physiological euphoria. However, ultimately the addiction becomes all-consuming and destructive. The addiction demands to be fed and destroys any incentive for productive pursuits. Just as a Meth addict will steal or become a prostitute to feed the habit, entitlements similarly warp our moral direction and our desire to be personally responsible. They are an attack on traditional American values.

We no longer expect that our federal government will be a servant of the people. We must acknowledge that we the people exist to feed the federal government. *Our addiction to federal largesse must be fed.*

Addiction to alcohol or drugs is incredibly difficult and painful to overcome, and requires unbelievable self-discipline and courage to break the bondage. The United States now faces the same painful choice. Either we muster the discipline and courage to break our addiction to entitlements, or we surely will destroy our national future.

Governmental Impact on Personal Responsibility and Our Family Structure

Personal responsibility is becoming a government-funded option. Governmental policy, regardless of the party in office, is creating a dependent class that looks to government for some or all of their income, food, shelter, medical care, childcare, education, elder care, etc. These products and services -- which are being bestowed by our benevolent government -- are now considered to be "rights".

As a current example, in the third 2008 presidential debate, then-candidate Obama, when answering a direct question, defined heath care as a "right". Almost all current media debate on health care issues begins with the presumption that it is a "right". The Democrats in Congress legislated this "right" into existence, in the Spring of 2010, by enacting their "health reform" bill.

When government determines that the provision of a good or service has become a "right", then logically, the government is now empowered to confiscate money by force from responsible, self-supporting individuals. It can then spend it on providing the goods or services to those who are incapable or unwilling to provide it for themselves. Since changes in human behavior result from the stimuli of reward and punishment, what human behavior would this encourage? Self-sufficiency or dependency?

Moreover, when government mandates the provision of these goods and services, they essentially conscript those who make the goods or provide the services, and force them to sell their products or expertise at the rate dictated by federal bureaucrats. It is likely that some number will refuse to do so, thereby creating scarcity and default rationing.

Now consider all the human needs and desires that, with very little debate, could be considered "rights", such as housing, education, elder care, transportation; the list grows quickly.   Now, extrapolate the dependency-generating effects of increasingly pervasive government-funded social programs and entitlements to take care of those ballooning "rights". Do you like where this is going?

Of course, the federal government already provides these products and services to some but not all citizens. In 2006, 61 million Americans were dependent on government for their daily housing, food and health care.[51]   Initially provided as a "social safety net" to the poor and elderly, these programs are creeping into the daily lives of more and more middle-class families. The 2010 health reform legislation authorizes insurance subsidies for families with incomes up to $88,000 per year[52]. State Children's Health Insurance Programs, or SCHIP, which vary by state, have provided generous benefits for children of middle-class families since enacted in 1997[53]. The Earned Income and Child Tax Credits provide cash welfare payments to middle class families making as much as $50,000 annually[54]. How do you say "No" to free benefits?

The Heritage Foundation has developed a mathematical *Index of Dependence on Government,* which tracks the growth of dependency in the U.S. The Index uses data drawn from federal programs which provide assistance or direct payments for housing, welfare, health care, retirement, higher education and rural / agricultural services. The programs included must result in a payment or assistance to an individual. The programs were chosen for their propensity to duplicate or replace support given to needy people by local organizations, neighborhoods, communities, and families.

As shown in the following graph, the Index (and thus the dependency of our population) has grown steadily in the last forty-seven years.[55] An update to the Index, released in June 2010, noted that *under the first year of the Obama Administration, the level of dependence on government has increased by an amazing 14%.* The Index has grown by 49% since 2001 alone.[56] These are not simply statistics. These figures portend a peril our nation has never faced -- internal dissolution and destruction of our core values.

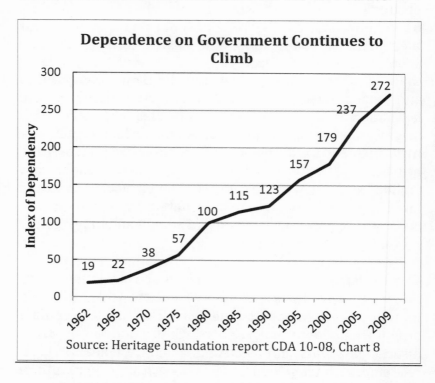

In a Heritage Foundation report authored by William Beach, the analysis is so profound and the implications so disturbing, that it is quoted directly:

"*Historically, private individuals and local entities have provided more assistance to needy members of society than they do today. Particularly during the 20th century, government gradually offered more and more services that were previously provided by self-help and mutual-aid organizations. Lower-cost housing is a good example. Mutual-aid, religious, and educational organizations have long aided low-income Americans with limited housing assistance, but after World War II, the federal and state governments began providing the bulk of low-cost housing. Today, the government provides nearly all public-housing assistance.*

Health care is another example of this pattern. Before World War II, Americans of modest income typically obtained health care and health insurance through a range of community institutions, some operated by churches and social clubs. That entire health care infrastructure has since been replaced by publicly provided health care insurance, largely through Medicaid and Medicare. Regardless of whether the medical and financial results are better today, the relationship between the people receiving health care assistance and those paying for it has changed fundamentally. Few would dispute that this change has negatively affected the total cost of health care and the politics of the relationships among patients, doctors, and hospitals.

Financial help for those in need has also changed profoundly. Local, community-based charitable organizations once provided the majority of the aid, which resulted in a personal relationship between the individuals receiving help and those in the community providing that assistance. Today, Social Security and other government programs provide much or all of the income to indigent and modest-income households. Unemployment insurance payments provide nearly all of the income to temporarily unemployed workers that was once provided by unions, mutual-aid societies, and local charities. Indeed, income assistance is quickly becoming a government program with little, if any, connection to the local civil society.

This shift from local, community-based mutual-aid assistance to government assistance has clearly altered the relationship between the person in need and the service provider. In the past, the person in need depended on help from people and organizations in his or her local community. The community representatives were generally aware of the person's needs and tailored the assistance to meet those needs within the community's budgetary constraints. Today, housing and other needs are addressed by anonymous government bureaucrats who have little or no ties to the community where the needy person lives.

Both cases involve a dependent relationship. However, the dependent relationship with elements of the civil society includes healthy expectations of the recipient's future civil viability or ability to aid another person in turn. The dependent relationship with the political system has no reciprocal expectations. The former relationship is essential to the existence of civil society itself. The latter is usually based on unilateral aid where the recipient's return to civil viability is not a factor. Indeed, the "success" of such government programs is frequently measured by the program's growth rather than the outcomes it produces. While the dependent relationship with civil society leads to a balance between the interests of the person and the community, the dependent relationship with the government runs the risk of generating political pressure from interest groups--such as health care provider organizations, local communities, and the aid recipients themselves--to expand and cement federal support."[57]

As just explained in the previous section, governmental provision of these goods and services becomes addictive. Human nature will ultimately prevail. Once given something over and over, we not only expect it to continue, we demand it. We become incapable of providing it for ourselves. Why should we? We have a "right" to it. Moreover, once government provides a good or service to one group, then others begin to think "Why them and not me too?" The Neo-totalitarians are glad to oblige -- just vote for them. They are happy to promulgate class warfare.

The use of government spending to provide charitable relief began with the New Deal. Some presidential administrations since that time created new government welfare programs. Every administration perpetuated what their predecessors had instituted. What originally *may* have been motivated by moral or humane considerations has now morphed into the political dispensation of dependency addiction. Neo-totalitarians are the dispensers and the ultimate winners in this game. Any opposition to the provision of governmental charity is now condemned by liberals, academics and the media as "mean-spirited", "heartless", or even "racist". However, as shown in the previous discussion on the impact of our national debt, we are now at the tipping point where economic reality and fiscal prudence must become a priority, or else we are literally condemning our posterity to penury. Either voluntarily or involuntarily, we as a nation will be forced to re-evaluate the role of government in the dispensation of charity.

James Madison, Founder and fourth President, emphatically wrote: *Charity is no part of the legislative duty of the government.*

Famous frontiersman and U.S. Congressman Davy Crockett experienced an epiphany concerning the unconstitutionality of governmental charity through the guidance of a constituent. This well-known anecdote, which Crockett called "*Not Yours to Give*", is repeated in full in Appendix I.

We are becoming a nation of supplicants. Personal responsibility, self-sufficiency, self-reliance, and individual pride are all American values that have built our great country. They are becoming irrelevant. They are being supplanted by the 'Nanny State' – the Neo-totalitarian federal government.

In the United States, our family structure has historically been the solid backbone of our country. It is a quintessential American value. Dependency-generating federal programs directly attack and destroy the American family.

Welfare, as it is currently structured, perpetuates single motherhood. Welfare programs create disincentives to marriage because benefits are reduced as a family's income rises. A mother will receive far more from welfare if she is single than if she has an employed husband in the home. For many low-income couples, marriage means a reduction in government assistance and an overall decline in the couple's joint income. Marriage penalties occur in many means-tested programs such as food stamps, public housing, Medicaid, day care, and Temporary Assistance to Needy Families.[58] As welfare rewards single parenthood, and as the number of single mothers grow, welfare continues to spiral upward, as shown in the Heritage Foundation chart below.[59]

Research has proven that to escape poverty and move up to the middle class, three prerequisites must occur. One must complete High School, work full time, and marry before you have children.[60] Current welfare programs seem almost intentionally designed to defeat all three. Think about the impact of that now, and on future generations, in terms of poverty, crime, and exponential demand for more social spending. Do we need a "change" we can believe in?

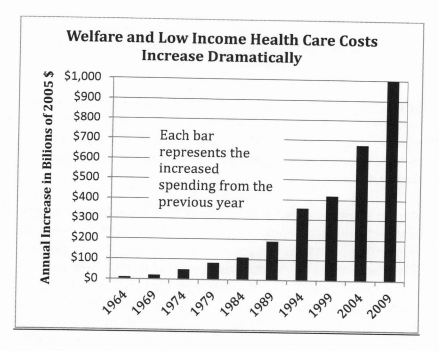

Consider this one fact that is both a consequence and a cause of our national decline in family stability. In the United States in 2008, across all races, 41% of babies were born out of wedlock.[61] Almost *half* of our newborns will grow up without both a mother and a father! Perhaps a handful of these children were planned and will be raised without aid from the government. But the overwhelming majority were not and will not. Cultural shifts enabled by governmental welfare programs have virtually eliminated any deterrence to unwed motherhood.

The decline in marriage and increase in unwed mothers is a significant factor in locking children into poverty, with associated social problems. A child born out of wedlock is seven times more likely to experience poverty than a child raised by married parents, and more than eighty percent of long-term child poverty occurs in broken or never-married homes. Children without fathers at home suffer in development, educational achievement, psychological well-being, and have a greater risk of delinquency and substance abuse.[62]

Americans have historically cherished our family-oriented culture as the bedrock of our society and the most effective teacher of values. In 21st century America, the paternalistic government is supplanting the family as supporter and teacher.

Recent anecdotal radio news report: "Study finds that the state is not doing enough to protect teens from date abuse".[63] How have we come to a place where the government would need to do this, and even worse, that we expect it to? Where are the Dads to protect their daughters or teach their sons? Is this the brave new world you really want to inherit?

The Federal Judiciary Prohibits Public Religious Expression

In April 2010, a Wisconsin federal judge ruled that the National Day of Prayer was unconstitutional. The judge explained that government can no more encourage citizens to pray than to "*fast during the month of Ramadan, attend a synagogue, purify themselves in a sweat lodge or practice rune magic."* [64] This is just one of the most recent attacks on our religious freedoms by an unrestrained federal judiciary.

Our country was founded as a Christian nation. Our founders believed that God was intimately involved in the birth of our nation, and that He responded to prayers for intervention and protection. For 200 years, our nation was guided by that belief. Former House Speaker Newt Gingrich has authored a superb small volume titled *Rediscovering God In America*, which documents the truth of this statement far better than I can.[65]

We have no government armed with power capable of contending with human passions unbridled by morality and religion. Avarice, ambition, revenge, or gallantry would break the strongest cords of our Constitution as a whale goes through a net. Our Constitution was made for a moral and religious people. It is wholly inadequate to the government of any other. --- John Adams, early patriot, Founding Father, and the second President of the United States

Of all the dispositions and habits which lead to political prosperity, religion and morality are indispensable supports. --- George Washington, Father of Our Country, in his Presidential Farewell Address

Is America perfect? Of course not. Any invention of mankind is flawed. But our Judeo-Christian beliefs are a vital reason that America is, and has been, a beacon for the world. No other country in recorded history has ever shed its blood as we have to liberate other peoples from tyranny *without a quid pro quo.* No other country has ever given the incredibly generous charitable aid that we give to the world, both privately and publicly.[66]

However, just within the last two decades, church / state separatists and "civil liberty" activists have been striving to make our religious heritage seem politically incorrect, and to make the public exercise of religion virtually illegal. Pursuant to this end, they manufacture a myth that any acknowledgement of this historical fact, by any government entity, is tantamount to our nation mandating a national religion. Incredibly, even though 76% of U.S. citizens identify themselves to be of Christian heritage[67], we allow this distortion by a mere handful of anti-religious zealots, aided and abetted by leftist organizations, primarily the American Civil Liberties Union.

As plaintiffs with virtually nothing to lose financially, these groups sue organizations, local governments or individuals, who in most cases cannot afford the cost of a defense. And beginning with the prohibition of public school prayer in the 1960's, the federal judiciary has been the Left's dependable accomplice. In those rare cases where defendants attempt to mount a defense, the federal court's politically correct precedent is to enforce the secularization of our nation. Our federal courts essentially defy not only the will of the vast majority of Americans, but ignore the most common sense interpretation of the Bill of Rights.

It seems to be working. The percentage of our people describing themselves as Christian is declining. In 1990, 86% of Americans so identified themselves; in 2008 the number had fallen to 76%. And the fastest growing religion in America is the Wiccan cult, essentially witches. Over the past eighteen years, the number of Americans identifying themselves as Wiccan or Pagan has grown by

8400%.[68] We have sunk to a national low point when one misguided individual can sue to prevent the President from taking the oath of office on a Bible and to stop prayer at his inauguration -- and we (our judicial system and our media) actually take the lawsuit seriously, and give credence to this demand. Sadly, this same President later reassured an international (and in particular Muslim) audience that "*America is not a Christian nation*".

Common sense would indicate that displaying a manger or a menorah on a town square, conducting a Christmas play or Passover celebration in an elementary school, or praying at a public gathering in no way can be construed as a law or regulation that the government requires its citizens to be Christian or Jewish. Neither does it imply that non-Christians or non-Jews, exposed to such an activity, must convert. The U.S. Constitution simply and clearly states that it prohibits a state-mandated religion, a *theocracy*. It does not prohibit its citizens from the free exercise of religion in a public (i.e. taxpayer-supported) setting.

Within the last few years, the progressive's secular attack has moved from restrictions (on public prayer, religious displays, etc.) to bold discriminatory stabs at Christian values and beliefs. For example, college administrations, bound by rigid political correctness codes, have refused to sanction and support Christian clubs on campus because they will not admit homosexuals or members of other faiths. In Massachusetts, Catholic adoption agencies shut themselves down rather than comply with the state's insistence that homosexual couples be allowed to adopt children. (Catholic adoption agencies in Britain face the same choice.) The board of the Public Broadcasting System (PBS), in June 2009, decided to begin enforcing a rule prohibiting all religious programming. The Left's attack is gradual but inexorable.

This attempted prohibition of any religious recognition by any governmental institution seems to focus primarily on Christianity. One would suppose this is because of the 76% statistic quoted above. Judaism, Islam, Hinduism often seem to get a pass in an effort to encourage "diversity". Celebrities embrace beliefs such as Scientology, Maoism or New Age Spirituality, and their talk show and gossip magazine discussions are viewed as fashionably avant-garde. However, anyone publicly professing a Christian faith outside of a strictly religious setting is labeled by the media and the political elite as "fundamentalist" or "evangelical", with associated connotations of inflexible dogma. Do you think this is accidental?

As much as the anti-religious front tries to deny the existence of God or His role in American life, they cannot refute the natural inclination of people to desire a spiritual relationship with a caring deity. It is innate in our being and has pervaded the history of mankind. More importantly, the precepts of religion provide us with a moral compass and parameters for a fulfilling life. Perhaps that is the underlying reason that those who desire for government to loom large in all facets of our existence seem so intent on removing all public traces of our religious heritage and practice. Neo-totalitarians desire for Americans to depend on the government, not on God.

Josef Stalin certainly understood this concept, and used the force of repression to implement it in the U.S.S.R. In fact, during the Cold War, Stalin said: *America is like a healthy body and its resistance is threefold: its patriotism, its morality, and its spiritual life. If we can undermine these three areas, America will collapse from within.*

The secularists are directly attacking the tenets espoused in the Declaration of Independence -- that our freedom comes from God, and thus is not dependent on any government. They are redefining one of our most basic foundational beliefs. Tragically, most Americans today think that our freedom comes from the beneficent federal government.

The sacred rights of mankind are not to be rummaged for among old parchments or musty records. They are written, as with a sunbeam, in the whole volume of human nature, by the hand of the Divinity itself and can never be erased or obscured by mortal power. --- Alexander Hamilton.

Gradual Decline in Our Country's Morals and Behavior Standards

At the risk of making a painfully obvious statement, mankind has always been capable of evil and self-destructive behavior. Throughout history, written laws and socially-accepted behavior standards have restrained and channeled our potential dark side. Within the last decades, American laws, and in particular, their judicial interpretation, are allowing and in some cases encouraging negative aspects of human interaction. Accepted standards of interpersonal behavior are becoming increasingly permissive, self-serving, dishonest, vulgar, rude and often self-destructive.

A recent survey by the Culture and Media Institute found that 74% of Americans surveyed felt that our moral values are weaker than twenty years ago. The two primary factors noted in the study were a decline in the influence of nurturing parents and families, and the influence of media messages, particularly television.[69]

A detailed epistle to conclusively document the slide in our moral standards would be far too much for this essay. Instead, try the random but hopefully enlightening sample below. In almost every example, there are no more than two degrees of separation between the moral decline and a governmental action or omission, be it judicial, legislative or regulatory. And before you dismiss them as simply prudish laments, consider their degrading impact on our society.

- Greed and dishonesty have become more widespread, even acceptable, causing corporate meltdowns (such as Enron) and financial calamities (such as the sub-prime mortgage implosion). Unfortunately, we are not talking about a handful of corrupt corporate executives; this mindset seems to be more pervasive. As evidence, consider the millions of individuals who eagerly applied for "liar loan" mortgages (in which the applicant could claim exaggerated incomes without proof). Moreover, with the exception of a few CEOs or CFOs who got a short jail sentence, such behavior is often not punished. Most of the execs walk away with Golden Parachutes, and dishonest homeowners are being bailed out by various government mortgage modification programs.

- From network television's 8 pm "family" hour: The immensely popular show *Friends* of a few years back depicted having children out of wedlock as cool and acceptable, with no mention of real-life consequences. The comedy show *30 Rock* blithely lampooned a fictional TV program titled "MILF

Island". If you do not know the acronym, then Google it , and be sure that millions of kids who saw this episode did the same thing. Ten o'clock p.m. network television shows now use cursing and sexual language that, twenty years ago, was limited to R-rated movies. The Federal Communication Commission has been delinquent in regulating television content.

- In a class by itself is the Comedy Channel cable TV show *South Park*. This animated series, which is on early enough to be seen by children, is crude beyond belief. It routinely crosses the line on vulgarity, sexuality and ethics, and has an unrelenting tone that mocks virtually everything. It defines "humor" in socially destructive terms.

- F-bombs, GD's, and explicit sexual language routinely appear in PG-13 movies, and moviegoers accept such language with the justification that "they hear worse than that at school".

- Internet pornography is available to anyone that can turn on a computer, and has inevitable degrading impacts on behavior norms and relationships. Even worse, the internet spreads the malignancy of child porn. Indeed, the anonymity of the internet seems to encourage "push the envelope" anti-social behavior. If you investigate *4chan.com*, you will see a perfect example.

- Middle school-age students are "sexting" nude pictures of themselves on their cell phones. A recent Pew Research study found that 15% of teenagers have received a nude or nearly nude picture of someone they know on their phones.[70]

- Every other year since 2002, Yale University, one of the country's premier Ivy League institutions, hosts Sex Week, which brings to campus an assortment of speakers and presentations. Of the 34 events scheduled for the 2010 event, eleven featured porn stars or adult film producers. Pornography is a highlight of the week, and this year's most heavily attended events were a live demonstration of Sado-Masochism and a detailed instruction session on oral sex.[71]

- State legislatures and courts battle over whether marriage is between a man and a woman, and an institution that has been the bedrock of human existence is under attack. As of this writing, 29 states have constitutional amendments and 36 states have enacted laws defining marriage as between a man and a woman only. However, many states have legalized a variety of civil unions or domestic partnerships. Five states allow homosexual marriage (New Hampshire, Vermont, Massachusetts, Connecticut. and Iowa).[72] It can be argued that the legal rights of homosexual partners can be guaranteed without legalizing their marriage. And that gay marriage advocates have a broader agenda concerning the American family.

- Federal and state legislators have serious discussions over the legal question of whether late term abortions are really "murder" of an unborn child, and thus should be allowable. Yet the imposition of the death penalty for horrendous crimes is portrayed as barbaric by liberal groups.

- Rap lyrics glorify violence and misogyny, yet they have become mainstream and impress a generation of youth of all races.

Does any of this matter? For a real-life example of how declining moral standards can cause internal rot and the eventual demise of an otherwise rich and powerful society, reference *The Decline and Fall of the Roman Empire.* Among several other factors, Edward Gibbons speculated that the decline of "civic virtue" contributed greatly to the collapse of the Empire. He wrote: *The decline of Rome was the natural and inevitable effect of immoderate greatness. Prosperity ripened the principle of decay; the causes of destruction multiplied with the extent of conquest; and as soon as time or accident had removed the artificial supports, the stupendous fabric yielded to the pressure of its own weight.*

The United States is not exempt from human nature. Despite our size, economic wealth and military strength, there are no guarantees that we are, or will remain, invulnerable.

Founding father Samuel Adams said it best: *A general dissolution of the principles and manners will more surely overthrow the liberties of America than the whole force of the common enemy.... While the people are virtuous they cannot be subdued; but once they lose their virtue, they will be ready to surrender their liberties to the first external or internal invader.*

The Destructive Effects of Labor Unions

The history of organized labor in America has been controversial. The influence that unions exert in the future will likely continue to be so. Collective bargaining, especially after it was empowered by New Deal legislation, has resulted in significant transfers of wealth from the owners of capital to the workers in the capitalist system. Undoubtedly, some consequences of this transfer were positive, and resulted in these workers and their families achieving a higher standard of living, and more importantly allowing their children to participate in educational levels that would not have been possible otherwise. Their education provided the springboard for economic prosperity for new generations.

The percentage of the U.S. workforce represented by unions grew from 7.4% in 1930 to a peak of 27.8% in 1970.[73] In 2009, this percentage of all workers stands at 12.4%. The rate of membership within the private sector is an amazingly low 7.2%, which is comparable to pre-Depression levels. The balance of present day union members are comprised of government workers, who are unionized at a rate of 37.4%, and growing.[74]

The reasons that private sector union membership declined beginning in the 1970's are myriad. Over time, many of the benefits that had been negotiated by unions had become legislated and regulated by the government, to the extent that workers began to question the need for union representation. Global competition forced U.S. companies to reduce labor costs to survive, so they negotiated for lower salaries and benefits or they out-sourced their labor to non-union states or countries. Younger workers, a growing segment of the workforce, do not see the need to belong -- less than 5% of union members are under 24 years old.[75] In many ways, labor unions in the private sector are becoming an anachronism.

Even though overall union membership may be decreasing, the influence of labor unions is still profound, especially in government. This influence has been accompanied by destructive forces which, on balance, have contributed to a decline in American rights and values, and pose a threat to our national future. Consider:

1. Beginning with the Great Depression, the Norris LaGuardia Act, the Wagner Act, and the traditional pro-labor slant of the National Labor Relations Board has tilted the collective bargaining equation in the favor of unions. The wages and benefits negotiated for fifty years in this country were often not constrained by competitive realities. Thus, especially in the manufacturing and construction sectors, and in those states that had union shop laws, wages and benefits became quite generous. Contractual work rules became restrictive, protective and counter-productive. Companies passed these costs on to the American consumer with relative ease, until the 1980's. With the advent of global competition, these union scale wages and benefits made American labor comparatively expensive, and union contractual work rules made American production less competitive.

The impact to our national economy was substantial. Our trade deficit has grown as we bought more foreign goods, but sold less to international markets. Whole sectors of our economy ultimately began to struggle. The steel, automotive and textile industries are examples. More than likely, there are other sectors with unwieldy labor costs that will impact our economy, and thus our financial freedom, for years.

2. As union influence wanes in the private sector, and their ability to negotiate is hamstrung by the economic reality of global competition, unions are shifting into survival mode,

and are redirecting their focus and their money. Rather than devote their energy toward issues of direct employee benefit, union funds are increasingly used to lobby, influence and empower Neo-totalitarian politicians, who have been the traditional allies of Big Labor. As these Neo-totalitarian elites continue their relentless quest for larger and more powerful government, more spending and less freedom, the financial and political support provided by union leaders poses a threat to our republic, and ironically to their own rank and file members.

3. As private sector union membership declines, labor has transitioned its organizing efforts toward a sector of employees whose numbers are growing and whose employers are in a monopolistic position, free of the demands imposed by economic supply and demand realities. Government at every level is becoming increasingly unionized. Public sector unions, notably the Service Employees International Union (SEIU), the American Federation of State, County and Municipal Employees (AFSCME) and the National Educational Association (NEA), spend enormous sums to support politicians who favor expanding government, raising taxes and, no surprise, increasing, protecting and enriching union employees. As discussed in previous sections of this work, our nation must come to grips with government spending and debt. The cost of government must go down, or our economy will decline. Public unions and their political allies will fight this, and thus imperil the future of freedom in America.

Moreover, since unionized government employees typically provide services for which there is no (or limited) private sector competition, disruption caused by work stoppages can disrupt crucial services (e.g., public transportation) or endanger the public (e.g., fire departments). One has only to look to the country of Greece to examine the danger inherent in widespread unionization of government workers. In the Spring and Summer of 2010, as the Greek government attempted to pull the country out of its debt-caused financial abyss by cutting spending, the unions protested and initiated strikes. Instead of attempting to be part of the solution, union members rioted and murdered innocent people.

4. American unions have a history of violence, intimidation, and racism. As Big Labor forms partnerships with government Neo-totalitarians to seek legal leverage, preferential treatment and largesse, these tactics are likely to flourish again. The Employee Free Choice Act (commonly known as Card Check) is desperately sought by union leaders and is supported by Neo-totalitarian politicians. This dangerous legislation would allow union organizing votes to be taken, not in a secret ballot, but by union organizers, confronting employees face-to-face. How can this not be considered intimidation? A foundational American right of privacy in a voting booth is under attack, simply to empower a Neo-totalitarian ally.

5. Of particular concern in the realm of public sector unions are the teachers unions, which represent about 75% of public school teachers. At this time in our history, education could not be more important for our national future, but our public educational system is achieving less and less, even as more tax dollars are being spent. Teachers unions fight every effort at being held accountable for improving educational results. They also are opposed to consideration and funding of alternative methods of education, such as charter schools and vouchers, that have proven to offer more effective results. They are clearly a threat to our country's traditional values regarding education.

6. The history of organized labor is inextricably tied to the Communist Party and Marxism. From the late 1800's and the birth of the International Working Men's Association, to the current International Workers of the World, the tenets of socialism have pervaded the rhetoric and tactics, and influenced the leaders of organized labor. The following excerpt concerns the International Workers of the World union versus the Starbucks Coffee Company:

The IWW Starbucks Workers Union is proud to celebrate the sixth anniversary of our campaign for fair wages, consistent scheduling, a healthier and safer workplace, and a voice on the job at the world's largest coffee chain. As we enter our sixth year of struggle, we leave behind us a year marked by the continued rapid deterioration of working conditions at Starbucks: the doubling of our health insurance costs, massive layoffs, reduced staffing, and the continued disregard of greedy company executives for the well-being of hard-working Baristas and their families. Even as Starbucks achieves record profits of $760.3 million in the last 12 months. This represents a profit of roughly $5,354 from each of Starbucks 142,000 workers. Rather than return the wealth of our labor to hard-working Baristas who are living in poverty, Starbucks executives issued the first-ever dividend to shareholders, further enriching the financial class that has driven our world to ruin in the worst economic crisis since 1929. However, even as conditions continue to worsen in corporate management's greed-fueled race to the bottom, our movement for justice at work continues to gather strength[76].

Even though this sentiment sounds like it was taken directly from the 1917 Russian Revolution manifesto, it was posted June 9, 2010. This is revealing in many ways. First, Starbucks has the reputation as a progressive, Green, young, hip, socially-conscious business. Yet the IWW portrays it as just another evil, greedy capitalist pig, in what has become a very tired and anachronistic tirade. Moreover, it represents the desperation of unions in general. As our economy transitions into service sector domination, organized labor is forced to attempt to organize these service employees, and focus on such non-vital issues as "consistent scheduling". The real danger from this Communist doctrine is that it is infecting the growing numbers of unionized government workers, and their vast bureaucratic influence upon our government structure.

Our Government Has Allowed Political Correctness to Run Amok

There are, at all levels, governmental agencies, panels and committees who will, with or without the basis of a complaint, investigate and prosecute individuals or businesses because someone was offended. Our judiciary at all levels will enforce financial sanctions against "offenders". Individuals and groups can destroy careers and corporations, not on the basis of a legitimate legal conviction of slander, but only because they were somehow offended, and therefore command media attention. It has become a game whereby the "offended" can complain and sue for fun and profit. Of course, our tort system encourages this.

Virtually every corporation or organization of any significant size has a department that exists solely to receive complaints from employees, who are encouraged to come forward if they are "harassed" or "offended" by fellow employees or management.

At one point, there were good intentions motivating the prohibition of truly offensive speech and behavior in the government crackdown on discrimination. But as often happens, we have now gone far beyond the bounds of common sense. Such that we now must deal with cases as absurd and surreal as the actual lawsuit filed because an airline passenger claimed she was offended by a nursery rhyme sung by a flight attendant to ask passengers to sit down.[77]   Nuisance lawsuits are not just aggravating -- defending and settling them increases the cost of whatever service is being provided to every other customer.

Moreover, the very real problem with political correctness in our society now is that it impedes the common sense solutions to tough problems, and more importantly can pose a threat to national security and individual safety. Consider the following examples.

- Frustrated by ineffective border control by the federal government, and spurred by the murder of a citizen by illegal immigrants, in April 2010, Arizona passed legislation which would empower state and local law enforcement to make a reasonable attempt to determine immigration status for persons detained for other legal reasons. Amid the immediate outrage from the Left, the most prominent objection was that it would subject Latinos in the state to "racial profiling". This is a *Catch 22* absurdity of the highest order. Virtually all the illegal immigrants in Arizona are Hispanic, but the state government is not allowed to check their status because they are Hispanic. How can we ever control our border with Mexico if the enforcement itself is considered politically incorrect? (As an interesting footnote to this situation, the Arizona law simply codifies and authorizes state enforcement of federal law which requires immigrants to carry appropriate documents with them which prove they may legally be in our country. Every national government in the world has similar laws, including Mexico. Act 67 of the Mexican Population Law states "Authorities, whether federal, state or municipal...are required to demand that foreigners prove their legal presence in the country, before attending to any issues".[78])

- The Fort Hood terrorist - murderer Nidal Hassan is a Major in the U.S. Army. For years, his superiors and fellow officers had become increasingly concerned about his escalating jihadist rhetoric and threats, yet for the most part they reported nothing because they feared being labeled as racist Islamophobes. Such a label apparently can hurt an officer's career. Incredibly, this Major continued to receive acceptable performance ratings. Even more infuriating, our national intelligence services knew for months that he was trying to contact Al Qaeda figures. In this case, political correctness killed twelve dedicated warriors and defenders of our liberty. What other threats exist that political correctness is currently hiding and protecting?

- The Transportation Security Agency refuses to employ the most common sense screening practices for fear they will be targeted with complaints of "racial profiling". It is ludicrous to subject the majority of air travelers to the security lines, metal detectors, bag checks, full body scans, pat-downs, etc. to protect us from Islamic jihadists. One has only to look to Israel, who faces terrorism on a daily basis from these same extremists, to understand that accepting the reality of who your enemy is can be extremely effective without handcuffing your entire population.

- The homeless. This sympathy-inducing term encompasses a wide spectrum of societal problems and masks them in political correctness. Certainly there are individuals and families that, for whatever cause or circumstance, find themselves in the terrible, hopeless position of not being able to afford shelter on a temporary basis. These Americans need and deserve our help. However, there also exists a more-or-less permanent population of homeless in almost every urban area whose homelessness is self-inflicted due to substance addiction, untreated mental illness or just laziness. These homeless are often intimidating and sometimes dangerous. Their lack of public hygiene and "urban camping" presence negatively affects quality of life for the responsible citizens with whom they share city spaces. Many are aggressive panhandlers. However, in city after city, political correctness has prevented enactment or enforcement of common sense ordinances to protect all citizens.

- In the Spring of 2010, a heretofore unknown group (which may of course be one individual) called the Military Religious Freedom Foundation, made a public complaint against the Pentagon for a planned speech by evangelist Franklin Graham (son of world renowned preacher Billy Graham) at a Pentagon National Day of Prayer event. Apparently, this group felt that Graham's past statements about Islam would cause his very presence in the building to offend Muslim workers. These Muslim workers would not, of course, be forced to attend the speech, but it was contended that their sensibilities would be harmed by simply being in proximity to Graham. Unbelievably, the Pentagon rescinded the invitation, denying thousands of our serving soldiers the opportunity to hear him, just to placate the absurd demands of a few.[79] Unfortunately, such politically correct lunacy is not isolated, it is all too common. How soon until the Day of Prayer itself is condemned by political correctness? (As an interesting aside, why do these groups insist on using terms like "freedom" or "liberty" in their names when their goals have nothing to do with exercising freedom and everything to do with restricting liberty?)

Perhaps the most damaging aspect of our current unrelenting politically correct atmosphere is that it inhibits the individual thought and expression that has been a hallmark of the American spirit. It seems to constantly promote "group think" by penalizing anyone voicing opinions considered politically incorrect. It definitely restricts our rights to free speech as defined in the Constitution.

Lastly, it restrains our sense of humor, and makes living life less enjoyable. Humor is a quintessential American trait. It lightens our load, and helps us deal with tragedy. However, we as a nation are becoming too intimidated to use humor in virtually any public setting, be it work or play, for fear of "offending". How many times have you heard one of these stories reported, and you said to yourself: "Please....just get a grip...it's a joke." We do not have to become a humorless nation.

The War on Capitalism

A nation can survive its fools, and even the ambitious. But it cannot survive treason from within. An enemy at the gates is less formidable, for he is known and carries his banner openly. But the traitor moves amongst those within the gate freely, his sly whispers rustling through all the alleys, heard in the very halls of government itself. For the traitor appears not a traitor; he speaks in accents familiar to his victims, and he wears their face and their arguments, he appeals to the baseness that lies deep in the hearts of all men. He rots the soul of a nation, he works secretly and unknown in the night to undermine the pillars of the city, he infects the body politic so that it can no longer resist. A murderer is less to fear. --- Cicero Marcus Tullius*

The capitalistic free-market economy of the United States, along with our abundance of natural resources, and the ingenuity and hard work of our population, has provided our citizens with a prosperity and standard of living that is the envy of the developed world. Historically, businesses large and small have had the basic intent to create wealth ....wealth for the entrepreneurs who took great risks to start their businesses, and wealth for the employees who worked in the businesses. And let us not forget the wealth for the governments that taxed the businesses and the employees.

Throughout our history, wealth creation has been valued and encouraged. It rewarded our national work ethic and our characteristic self-responsibility. It benefited everyone in America directly or indirectly. Our public infrastructure, our social systems (education, health, etc.), our personal standard of living, our hygiene and safety, our leisure time, our longevity....all have been immensely enhanced because we are a wealthy *capitalistic* country.

In terms of financial aid, from both governmental and private sources, to U.S. citizens and to the nations of the world, we are the most altruistic and generous country that has ever existed.[80] This could not be were it not for the wealth generated by our free market economy.

With the advent of the Progressive Era in the late 19th and early 20th centuries, there has been a war on capitalism from the Left. Academics, journalists and political activists in America, fueled by the Communist Revolution in Russia and socialist advancements in Europe, began the fight against capitalistic free markets on our home shores. The mantra was (and is) that capitalism creates inequality, and therefore is inherently evil.

In America, we as a society have rejected this dogma, and have traditionally believed that what should be equal is the freedom of opportunity. This stems from our Judeo-Christian roots, whereby it was a firmly held religious belief of our Founding Fathers that we have been granted the blessing of "free will" from God, to make of it whatever we may, thus establishing the concept of an unalienable right. Americans have historically held that freedom, by its very definition, will result in some people having more wealth than other people, and we have believed that to be fair and good, not "evil". We have witnessed the truth of the adage: "A rising tide lifts all boats".

In some instances, the early battles against capitalism included worthy causes to improve the working conditions or product quality of unscrupulous manufacturers. However, the point must be made that while freedom does allow people who manage businesses to make bad decisions, it is not the freedom or the capitalist system that is inherently bad, it is the individuals that made the harmful decisions who are bad. Dangerous and misguided decisions, made through the frailty of the human mind, are by no means limited to free market systems. One typical example (out of hundreds) is the mismanagement of the U.S.S.R.'s collectivist agricultural program, which directly resulted in the Famine of 1922, causing the death of five million souls.[81]

For the most part, in the early 20th century, attacks on American capitalism were directed from fringe elements, and were made with words, and not barricades in the streets. The mainstream citizens of America did not take these ideas seriously...they were living the benefits of capitalism. Radicals could be ignored, they were harmless.

Realizing that an overt revolution was not going to occur, socialist progressives took a different path. Rather than attack from outside the system, they would infiltrate the system and gradually change it from within. The covert war on capitalism began in earnest with the New Deal. The politicians and policy makers who came to power with Franklin Roosevelt were not devotees of free market capitalism, but were committed to evolutionary change in the fundamental principles of American governance and structure. They believed that free markets must be subordinated to government, and they used the crisis of the Great Depression to fire the first destructive salvos in their war on capitalism.

In the ensuing years, our government has become the regulatory arbiter of our economy. But, even as this was occurring, our political leaders, academics and media did not openly attack capitalism. After all, for most of these intervening years, we were officially in a "Cold War" with communism. Open, outright disparagement of our free market system would have resulted in a population confused by cognitive dissonance.

However, that restraint from the Left is now gone. Our memory of the Cold War against Communism is fading. In the 21st century, the gloves have come off. By words and deeds, the Neo-totalitarians, energized and empowered by their political victories in 2006 and 2008, seemed determined to drive a stake into the heart of American capitalism.

Consider first the deeds.

- In response to criminal acts of one corporation (Enron), our Congress passed the Sarbanes-Oxley Act. This incredibly burdensome legislation places onerous accounting and compliance regulations, along with criminal penalties, on virtually every business of any significance in America. This act inhibits our international competitiveness at a time of ever-increasing global competition, and costs businesses literally billions of dollars to comply, with minimal benefit. These costs have, of course, been passed on as increased prices to consumers. In typical governmental overzealousness, the regulations are aptly compared to using a sledgehammer to swat a mosquito.

- In 2009, the Obama Administration "saved" General Motors by firing its CEO and forcing the company into a government sponsored bankruptcy. During the expedited bankruptcy proceedings, our government literally cheated the company's bond holders, thereby setting a very dangerous precedent for future investors. Our government essentially rewarded a political ally (the automotive labor unions) with partial ownership of General Motors, even though they were a culpable partner in the destruction of this industry.

- In January 2010, the Obama Administration proposed the Financial Crisis Responsibility Fee. If approved by Congress, this fee would impose a 10 year, $90 billion tax on the largest financial institutions, ostensibly to recoup the costs of the 2008 bailout. Ironically, these same financial institutions have already paid back almost all the funds provided to them in the TARP, with interest. The federal government has made a substantial profit from selling the bank stock it acquired in exchange for the loans. In an absurd twist, the fee would not affect General Motors, Chrysler, AIG, Fannie Mae and Freddie Mac. Of these, only GM has made a small effort to repay its bail-out funds. These firms will probably never be able to repay the billions in aid they received.[82]

- In 2010, Health Reform legislation was passed by Democrats in defiance of the clearly expressed demands of the majority of Americans, using bullying tactics, unethical deals and bold lies (e.g., "it will reduce the deficit"). This horrendous legislation, which no member of Congress had the time to read and understand, will inject the heavy hand of the federal government directly into a sector that represents almost 20% of our economy. The repercussions and unintended consequences are almost unimaginable.

- Following quickly on the heels of their health care "success", Democrats in Congress passed another law, comprising thousands of pages, to add even more regulation and bureaucracy to the financial industry, which is already one of the most regulated sectors of our economy. This is being done to "protect" us from another meltdown, even though numerous laws and multiple watchdog agencies that already exist failed to predict and prevent the Great Recession we are still living through. Again, no member of Congress can possibly grasp the complexity of such massive legislation, not to mention truly anticipate the consequences to our nation's economy, both intended and unintended.

- The Obama Administration created a "Pay Czar" who has inserted governmental oversight into what has heretofore been a private market decision. This czar has restricted pay and bonuses for executives of bailed-out corporations. Even more invasive is Section 956 of the 2010 Financial Reform Act which requires the SEC, the FHA and other agencies to develop regulations on all incentive based compensation at all covered financial institutions with at least $1 Billion in assets.[83]

- The Obama Administration's response to the BP Oil Spill in the Gulf of Mexico in the Spring and Summer of 2010 was revealing. On June 4, Obama warned BP officials against "nickel-and-diming" the economic victims of the oil spill. In his statement, he condemned the company for spending billions of dollars to pay out dividends, and boldly insinuates that BP will probably be unethical or unfair in dealing with damage claims.[84] In reality, as of the first week in June, BP had already paid out $48 million on 18,000 claims -- and not one claim had been denied.[85] In political over-kill designed solely to allow Obama to appear decisive in crisis, he declared a moratorium on new and existing offshore deepwater drilling. In reality, this action will do far more harm than good. As rigs are shut down and relocated, it will cost thousands of jobs, directly harm thousands of families, will disrupt our domestic oil supply, and will hurt state government's tax collections at a time when state budgets are strapped. The logical, reasonable, common-sense response would have been a thorough inspection of off shore rigs to determine if all safety practices are being scrupulously followed, and shut down individual violators. Instead, the Administration willfully impugns all and damages all, and in the process sends this message: "Businesses are bad and must be punished". In a June sound bite that went viral, Obama pledged to find out what happened, so he would know whose "ass to kick". It certainly appears that the asses he chose first were the businesses in the oil industry and the working people in the Gulf.

Now consider the words.

- In numerous sound bites during the debate over health care, President Obama, House Speaker Pelosi, and Senate Majority Leader Reid used the term "evil" to describe health insurance companies. This is pure propaganda of the vilest sort. These companies provide an invaluable product which helps millions of Americans, while making a very modest 3-5% profit. (They are, after all, profit seeking businesses.)

- President Obama: "*I did not come here to help out fat cat bankers*".

- President Obama: "*I will not allow the insurance companies to run roughshod over the American people*".

- Candidate Obama: "*I just want to spread the wealth a little.*"

- Vice President Biden: "*We all need some skin in the game*".

- Obama, again: "*The financial meltdown dramatically showed the dangers of too little government, when a lack of accountability on Wall Street nearly led to the collapse of our entire economy.*"

- Obama, again: "*I want to be clear. We're not trying to push financial reform because we begrudge success that's fairly earned. I mean, I do think at a certain point you've made enough money.*"

- President Obama's address on health care to the Joint Session of Congress September 9, 2009: *If you misrepresent what's in this plan, we will call you out.*

- Rep. Charles Rangel : "*If we've got to have a battle, if we've got to have a fight, if we've got to deal with terrorists, whether they're in the Middle East or whether they're in Wall Street....*"

- When large corporations had the temerity to announce that the Health Reform Act would cost them hundreds of millions in lost tax credits, and would likely result in reducing or eliminating insurance benefits to retired employees, Congressional Democrats were infuriated and threatened hearings and investigations, somehow insinuating that these businesses had behaved egregiously. When reminded that we still have free speech in this country, and that the financial adjustments were required by the Act, the legislators withdrew their threat.

- And in April 2010, the political theater of the Goldman-Sachs Congressional hearings vilified and scape-goated an industry that participated in the meltdown of 2007-2008, but hardly was the proximate cause. As will be documented in a subsequent section of this book, that dubious honor belongs to the U.S. Government.

- The attacks are not just from the left-leaning politicians. The media has been relentless in reporting the propaganda to the masses. How many times have we heard sound-bites vilifying a "Wall Street" that victimized "Main Street"?

- The writers and producers of American films often join the ranks of the Leftists in targeting our free market capitalist system for propagandistic abuse, both subliminally and overtly. The reader can probably remember several films with an underlying plot message that American businesses are uniformly uncaring, selfish, greedy and predatory. No movie in recent production portrays this theme more audaciously than the 2010 hit *Avatar*. This blockbuster was supremely creative and entertaining, but the film's not-so-subtle message portrays an evil, unscrupulous mega-corporation as the villain out to rape the natural resources of planet Pandora and wipe out the indigenous inhabitants simply because they stand in the way of profits. Director James Cameron's vision of corporate motives is outdated by at least one hundred years. Any American citizen who works for a modern American corporation knows full well that they strive mightily to comply with the myriad complex (and often conflicting) federal laws and regulations that would prevent any of the abuses shown in the movie. Moreover, virtually all businesses of any size realize that it is to their direct financial benefit to be caring, generous citizens of the communities, cities and states where they operate. They help civic and charitable efforts of all kinds with direct financial aid, by allowing employees to contribute support on work time, and by encouraging them to do so on personal time. The Hollywood myth is not only overwhelmingly untrue, it is harmfully warping how impressionable minds view capitalism.

- And then, of course, there is Michael Moore. His latest work, *Capitalism, A Love Story*, is a pseudo-documentary which decries our free market as existing solely to benefit the rich while condemning millions to poverty. The movie ends with this conclusion: *"Capitalism is an evil, and you cannot regulate evil. You have to eliminate it and replace it with something that is good for all people and that something is democracy."* Mao Tse Tung could not have said it better.

Words have power. Today, most Americans still believe in our free market system. A March 2010 Pew Research survey asked if: "Most people are better off in a free market economy even though some people are rich and some are poor." In the United States, 68% agreed, versus 24% who disagreed. In an interesting counterpoint, 84% of those surveyed in the Peoples Republic of China agreed.[86]

The actions and the words of the war on capitalism will ultimately have an impact, if not now, then on future generations. And as will be shown in the next section, our future generations are being fed an academic diet of socialism in our universities.

This book is not intended as a detailed defense of our capitalist economy versus other forms. Such a treatise is unnecessary. History provides a clear and unequivocal answer. All other economic models have been tried and failed (or are failing). Modern totalitarian economies do not survive.

Stalin's iron-fisted centralized control drove the Soviet nation to starvation. Their collectivist manufacturing infrastructure was inadequate to defend the country from Germany in WW II. America, as the Arsenal of Democracy, provided the industrial might to allow the U.S.S.R. to survive. Stalin was supplanted by communistic politburos, which were no more successful at lifting the country from mediocrity. Ultimately, their totalitarian economic system finally imploded in the 1980's leading to the dissolution of the U.S.S.R. and the birth of economic and personal freedom.

Mao's regime was even more repressive, secretive, and exerted absolute control of the national economy of China (that is, anything beyond the individual subsistence farmer). Mao's dictatorial system, after killing and starving millions, transitioned to a communist central committee after his death. It failed to bring the nation out of the dark ages. Amazingly, in the last decade, the Chinese government, while still saving face with official homage to Mao and his Little Red Book, has embraced the wealth production that is only possible from the incentives of capitalism. By encouraging private business investment and entrepreneurship, Chinese government officials have truly begun to lift their population out of poverty, and improve their living standards and conditions. China, in ten short years, has become our economic rival for global resources and our greatest competitor in world markets.

So called socialistic democracies are no more successful. Examine the European model our progressive elite seems so eager to adopt. Greece is in utter chaos from their economic collapse. Great Britain faces its gravest fiscal crisis since WW II. France's socialistic isolationism has created an unmotivated society in malaise. Ireland, in late 2010, is on the verge of economic collapse and will require bail-outs from its European partners. Italy, Spain and Portugal are all in debt-fueled decline. In June 2010, newly elected British Prime Minister David Cameron announced that his nation's finances were worse than feared and will require sacrifices to *"our very way of life"*.[87] The British Treasury chief then created an austerity package which will see welfare payments and spending programs slashed, and said: *"We've had to pay the bills of past irresponsibility. We've had to relearn the virtue of financial prudence."* [88]

Totalitarianism of whatever degree has simply not worked. It rewards the worst aspects of human nature. In example after example, from Zimbabwe to North Korea to Cuba, we see the human tragedy wrought by an economic system that simply is destined to collapse. And yet we as a nation are allowing ourselves to be led straight into the same tragic outcome. What arrogance, what hubris to believe that the United States will be different.

There stands before the world one great and inescapable conclusion: Freedom leads to prosperity. Freedom replaces the ancient hatreds among the nations with comity and peace. Freedom is the victor. General Secretary Gorbachev,

if you seek peace, if you seek prosperity for the Soviet Union and Eastern Europe....Come here to this gate. Mr. Gorbachev, open this gate! Mr. Gorbachev, tear down this wall!
--- President Ronald Reagan

The Takeover of Our Colleges by Academic Neo-totalitarians

That's not to say there isn't a range of political viewpoints on campus. But those on the right of the University (of Oregon) faculty are basically Social Democrats, with the left represented by an anti-capitalism that flirts openly with Marx. --- Dan Lawton, columnist for the University of Oregon's Daily Emerald Newspaper

The liberal Left has essentially taken monopolistic control of the faculty at our country's universities and colleges, both private and state-funded institutions. This phenomenon has been observed and reported for years. In multiple studies, the overall percentage of professors who self-identify themselves as liberal, averages about 70%. Registered Democrats on faculty overwhelmingly exceed registered Republicans. The more elite the university, the more liberal the faculty. Harvard has been called the "Kremlin on the Charles". In certain disciplines, such as the Humanities, Political Sciences, Education, Journalism or Social Work, there are virtually no Conservative-leaning academics.[89]

The reason this bias continues has also been studied, and most research concludes that it is not overt discrimination, but simply self-selection. Established, tenured liberals tend to mentor like-minded students, encourage them to pursue an academic career, subtly guide their research and thinking, and reward certain conclusions. Other studies suggest that the tenure system itself isolates professors and protects them from the necessity of confronting competing opinions. Existing tenured professors control who is awarded tenure at their institutions, so naturally they tend to embrace those who talk and write as they do.[90]

My own experience indicates that almost everyone with extreme liberal views has deeply intertwined their sense of self-worth as a person with their liberal ideology. They do not take kindly to being challenged. Common sense would tell us that this type of personality would gravitate to a position where their views would not be questioned, and thus their self-worth would be most secure.

Even more interesting is how this trend began. It is safe to say that the takeover began in earnest in the 1970's. Prior to that period, most professors were stodgy and perhaps eccentric, but not radical Leftists. However, after almost forty years of transition, we find the one-sidedness of political thought on campus that is revealed in current research. My own opinion is that it is a direct result of the political opposition and protest of the Vietnam War in the late Sixties and early Seventies. These protests started and flourished on college campuses, which, as a nurturing safe haven from the real world, allowed students to passionately pursue the protests while being somewhat insulated from any consequences. These young people ingested radicalism and came to believe that social democracy was clearly a better choice than the status quo government that had led us into the quagmire of Vietnam. Because the academic environment protected, and in some cases encouraged, their radicalism, they tended to remain and formed the seeds for the current Neo-totalitarian academia.

The fascinating irony to this ongoing bias is that it so utterly hypocritical. College campuses, like no other places in America, have the most rigid codes enforcing diversity of race, gender, sexual persuasion and age. This fervent quest for diversity has been elevated to a religion on our campuses. Our institutions of higher learning claim to be a bastion of free thought and a home to searchers for truth in its purest form. However, when it comes to diversity of political thought and opinion, as these studies show, our campuses are anything but diverse. In fact, political correctness is mandated with dictatorial thoroughness. In researching this topic, many anecdotal examples were found of faculty members' liberal biases intimidating and restricting student participation, and in some cases, penalizing political opinions that differed from the academic group-think.

It is probably fair to state that overwhelmingly liberal professors teach as they believe. Therefore, we have two generations (Gen X and the Millennials) that have been and are currently being indoctrinated in these liberal cauldrons. It is only the unique and extremely confident student that can openly challenge the opinions and thus the authority of their professors by offering conservative viewpoints. Most students conform to and regurgitate what they are fed. Some do so simply to achieve a grade. Many are indeed convinced and converted.

One has only to examine the documented leftist slant of the current "mainstream" media to observe the results of indoctrinating journalism students with the liberal tenets of their professors, and then sending them into the workforce.

This is one of the greatest challenges that Conservatives face. As will be discussed in a subsequent section of the book, the Millennial generation is absolutely the key to our national future. Their votes will determine what kind of America emerges in the next decades. Hard working parents send their children to college in the comfortable notion that they are preparing them for a successful future. In all too many cases, they are sending young, malleable minds to be influenced by a socialist and secular faculty that wants nothing to do with a "center-right" America.

The following Question and Answer excerpt is from an interview with a 25 year old recent graduate who was an active Conservative on campus, and actually filed a lawsuit (and won) challenging the politically correct restrictions on student speech and activity. It is chilling:

Q: *You blogged recently that "college campuses have become the most intolerant environment for free speech over the last few decades, with conservative students...in the crosshairs of hostile leftist professors." Do you really believe that?*

A: *I experienced it! I'm Jewish, but there is anti-Israel sentiment on campus and.....selective enforcement of speech codes, and even plain old double standards when it comes to people of faith, mainly Christians. The tactics that they use are extremely toxic.*[91]

Part Three:
The Fallacy of Paternalistic Totalitarianism

That government is best which governs least.

Government, even in its best state, is but a necessary evil; in its worst state, an intolerable one.
--- Thomas Paine

Government Fails More Than It Succeeds

The American federal government has grown exponentially since the New Deal. Federal spending since 1970 has increased approximately 1,700%.[92] Our government is absolutely monolithic. It monitors, regulates or influences every aspect of our lives. It consumes vast resources. It wastes more money than most nations will ever have. And, as described above, it is in many ways destroying the value system that built our country and that most of our citizens cherish

But, at its core, there is a fallacy which invalidates paternalistic totalitarianism. Government at any level is almost never the most efficient user of resources or provider of services. It has no incentive for effectiveness or efficiency.   It is almost always monopolistic in its approach. The type of services and the manner in which they are provided by the government are usually determined, or at best, highly influenced by, political expediency and the quest for political advantage. Once empowered, government is incredibly slow to respond to changing conditions or demands. It is unconcerned with poor "customer" service, and is loath to recognize and correct its mistakes.

Government's view of the economy could be summed up in a few short phrases: If it moves, tax it. If it keeps moving, regulate it. And if it stops moving, subsidize it.
--- President Ronald Reagan

History has proven that government can rarely solve complex economic or societal problems; it usually makes them worse, or creates brand new ones through the law of unintended consequences.   However, once in place, government bureaucracies become self-sustaining and virtually impossible to remove.

No government ever voluntarily reduces itself in size. Government programs, once launched, never disappear. Actually, a government bureau is the nearest thing to eternal life we'll ever see on this earth!
--- President Ronald Reagan

Why do we as an electorate continue to empower a political class that promulgates a paternalistic totalitarian system that essentially does not work for its citizens? Common sense and honesty compel us to admit that what we are doing is illogical and self-defeating. It cannot come as any surprise that a Pew Research Center survey released in April 2010 found that 78% of the Americans surveyed do not trust our federal government and believe that the federal bureaucracy cannot solve the nation's problems. *Nearly one half said the government negatively affects their daily lives.* Favorable ratings for both parties, as well as for Congress, have reached record lows. [93]

Consider the following examples of government ineptitude, ineffectiveness, waste and unintended damage. These are just a juicy sampling from the annals of federal actions, solutions, programs and services. A book could be written just on this subject alone and not scratch the surface.

1. From 1920 to 1933, the 18th Amendment and the Volstead Act prohibited the production, importation or sale of alcoholic beverages. This experiment in government-enforced morality destroyed thousands of jobs in the legitimate alcohol-producing industry, but had virtually no impact on the actual consumption of alcohol, nor any of the "problems" it was intended to solve.

It did create massive, underground smuggling and distribution systems, which paid no taxes. It resulted in increased law-enforcement expenditures. Illegal importation of alcohol increased the power of organized crime and increased the violence associated with it (which continues to this day), and contributed greatly to corruption of government officials at all levels. This legislation was so horrendously ineffective, destructive and unpopular that it only took 13 years to repeal it. Legislative (and executive and judicial) actions that are merely somewhat ineffective or inefficient are almost never repealed.

2. The U.S. Post Office, now euphemistically renamed the U.S. Postal Service, is a heavily unionized government agency, which, until the last two decades, had no competitive forces to rein in the wages, staffing levels and work rules that were "negotiated" by Post Office bureaucrats.   The USPS was incredibly bloated, over-staffed, inefficient and entirely complacent.   In other words, it was a typical unit of government. The only form of cost control was the amount of its annual federal budget increases. It could raise its prices (of stamps) without real supply and demand consequences.

As a result of these problems, this bureaucratic behemoth began to face real-world competition. The United Parcel Service and Federal Express (FedEx) began taking huge chunks of market share in package shipping. The USPS was worried, but not enough to make radical changes. After all, it has an enforced monopoly on first class mail.

Now a true strategic threat has emerged from the internet. In practices that evolved over the last fifteen years, individuals and businesses can send email instead of letters, can pay bills on-line rather than mail checks, and can even download and watch movies on a computer, rather than mail a DVD. In an almost unprecedented occurrence, American citizens have alternatives to monopoly government. Private enterprises in a genuine capitalistic environment face these conditions continuously, and must improve and evolve, or they fail. The USPS, of course, merely requests more federal subsidy, attempts to reduce services provided and raises the price of postage, as it loses billions and continues its death spiral.

3.   The Endangered Species Act is the poster-child of legislative good intentions, morphing into unintended consequences and regulatory overkill.   Passed virtually unanimously in 1973, at President Nixon's urging, this law rode the 1970's wave of environmental legislation, as the nation seriously came to grips with decades of pollution and damage.   Section 29a summarizes its lofty purpose: "all species of fish, wildlife and plants are of aesthetic, ecological, educational, historical, recreational and scientific value to the nation and its people".   The ESA granted the power to deem plants and animals "endangered" or "threatened", and thus prevents the *taking* or destruction of the species, or any modification of their habitat, whether on public or private lands.   The designation as "endangered" can be initiated by the Fish and Wildlife Service, or can be requested through petition of individuals and organizations. The Act does not require such a designation to include any assessment of the economic or social consequences to humans (although subsequent implementation has attempted to inject such evaluations into the process).

The ESA has two fundamental flaws: First, it penalizes private landowners, if endangered species are found to inhabit their property, by restricting the use of the land without compensation. Second, the ESA seems incapable of balancing the needs of humans with the value of the species in question.   There have been several highly publicized cases that are emblematic of the inevitable conflicts arising from these laws.

- The TVA's Tellico Dam project was intended to provide hydroelectric power to millions of people, resulting in short-term economic benefit and long-term water management. It was derailed because it, allegedly, impacted the habitat of a minnow-sized fish called the Snail Darter.

- Listing the Northern Spotted Owl as endangered, ultimately resulted in the Pacific Northwest Plan (aided by the intervention of President Clinton) which placed over 25 million acres of federal land under eco-system management. This action substantially reduced the timber harvested, and required economic aid for thousands of unemployed loggers and their families.

- Private landowners in Riverside County CA were prevented from removing underbrush to create firebreaks so that the Stephens Kangaroo Rat would not be disturbed. In the ensuing fires, several homes burned, as did the rat's habitat.

- More recently, another small and seemingly insignificant fish, the Delta Smelt, has caused severe reductions in the amount of irrigation water available to the farmers of California's central valley agricultural region during a terrible drought. Consequently, in 2009, unemployment in these communities ranged from 20-40% and 250,000 acres of farmland lay fallow or dying. The region's agricultural output has declined by billions of dollars.

- The designation of endangered is becoming increasingly politicized. The Polar Bear is now categorized as "endangered" because its habitat seems to be changing, presumably due to global warming, although it is not at all clear that their population is declining or even threatened.

The ESA has been tremendously successful at empowering environmental groups and regulators, and enriching litigators, but has been far less successful at actually protecting endangered species. While there have been notable examples of animal and plant populations being revived (the American Alligator, the Bald Eagle, the Gray Wolf, the Gray Whale, the Grizzly Bear), the vast majority of the nearly 1,900 species on the list remain endangered, and fewer than 50 have ever been delisted. According to a Wall Street Journal article on the ESA's 30th anniversary, more species were delisted due to extinction than recovery.[94]

4. The U.S. Department of Energy is a spectacular example (among many) of a federal organization created to achieve a mission of critical national importance, then being unable to successfully complete the mission, but instead transforming itself into a self-sustaining, ever-expanding bureaucracy with vague goals and huge budgets. Formed as a cabinet-level department in 1977 by President Carter, the DOE was assigned one overriding goal: dramatically reduce our country's reliance on foreign sources of petroleum. This mission stemmed from the oil crises of the 1970's in which our foreign suppliers, led by OPEC, withheld supplies, raised prices and wreaked havoc in our economy.

How well has the DOE accomplished this task? In 1973, the U.S. imported about 35% of its petroleum from foreign suppliers. In 2006, we imported 60% from foreign countries. In 2008, due to price spikes and then a recession, our importation reduced slightly to 57%. Over *half* of our oil supply comes from outside the U.S. The chart below graphically demonstrates this increase in dependence.[95]

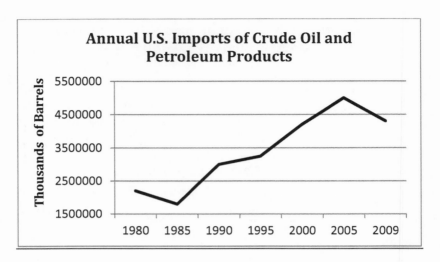

Even more alarming is the nature of the countries that supply our oil. Twenty-one percent of our oil comes from nations in the Persian Gulf region, 22% comes from African nations, and 11% comes from Venezuela[96]. These sources are very or somewhat politically unstable, and some are downright hostile to the U.S. Our national economy could be devastated and our personal freedom could be restricted from any significant reduction in supply from any of these nations. Moreover, we are sending billions of dollars to countries that are not necessarily our allies on the world stage.

Having failed to achieve its mandate, the DOE now has a generic, five-part mission[97]. Are they more successful? Let's analyze each.

- "Promote America's energy security through reliable, clean and affordable energy". On providing energy security by ending our dependence on foreign oil, the DOE is a complete failure. On developing "clean" energy, the DOE has spent billions since the 1980's on renewable sources of electricity, and on alternative sources of transportation energy. The 2009 Stimulus Bill devotes $37 billion dollars over two years to the DOE to research "green" energy. Today, alternative sources of electricity or transportation are still not cost effective (when compared to the major sources) and are not in widespread usage. It is easy to question whether the agency desires a breakthrough, or simply a continuation of the chase. Indeed, the DOE was excoriated by its own Inspector General in a 2009 audit which found that the agency did not even turn off its own computers to save energy, and avoid $1.5 million per year in electric bills.[98] At least they have managed to maintain the Strategic Petroleum Reserve without losing it.

- "Ensure America's nuclear security" The DOE is responsible for nuclear weapons design, testing, production, transportation, storage and disposal. For the most part, they accomplish this task. There have been no losses of nuclear material, at least that have been made public. However, there have been several instances of investigations into lax security, particularly at the Los Alamos National Laboratory and the Savannah River complex. Some of the investigations found that employee "whistleblower" accusations were minimized and or covered up by DOE management. There was also the highly publicized case of Wen Ho Lee, whom the DOE accused of stealing nuclear secrets for China. After a botched investigation and prosecution, Mr. Lee was released and subsequently won a $1.6 million civil settlement from the agency. It is still unclear (at least publicly) whether the secret information was transferred.[99] The one area of nuclear security in which the DOE has, without question, failed miserably has been in providing a permanent storage facility for spent nuclear fuel from commercial generating plants. Electric utilities have paid billions into a fund to provide such storage. After spending $10 Billion on construction of the Yucca Mountain storage facility, Secretary Chu (the Obama appointee) simply announced it would never be used. No other option is even being discussed at this time. (Simultaneously, in a counterintuitive and illogical policy move, the Obama Administration is encouraging the construction of new nuclear plants by guaranteeing their financing.)

- "Strengthen U.S. scientific discovery, economic competitiveness and improve quality of life through innovations in science and technology". From the viewpoint of money spent, the DOE is a huge success. They grant billions each year and provide 40% of the national funding for research in the physical sciences and renewable energy.[100] However, we as a nation are losing our competitive edge to India and China, and are spending more for electricity, petroleum, natural gas, and virtually every other source of energy.

- "Protect the environment by providing a responsible resolution to the environmental legacy of nuclear weapons production". The mission is to clean up the sites that made nuclear weapons. A 2000 staff report for the House of Representatives Committee on Energy and Commerce found, "*After years of poor management and a lack of integration of clean-up programs, it is clear that the DOE has squandered hundreds of millions of dollars on technologies that have not proved useful for the clean-up mission, and the agency and its clean-up contractors have failed to effectively use the technologies the agency produced......Remarkably, DOE was unable to readily provide this information (on cost and effectiveness of cleanup techniques) because it simply did not keep track of these basic programmatic performance measures."*[101] Are you reassured?

- "Enable the mission through sound management" If the failures discussed above were not enough to make this goal sound like a sad joke, consider that there have been several recent reports from the U.S. General Accounting Office that state: *"DOE's contract management, including both contract administration and project management, continues to be at high risk for fraud, waste, abuse and mismanagement."* [102] Your tax dollars at work.

The DOE had a budget of $31 billion in 2009 and is authorized to spend $24 Billion in 2010 -- not including the extra billions from the Stimulus Act. It has 16,000 full time federal employees and 100,000 contractors.[103] Please answer the following question. If a private corporation were spending this exorbitant amount of money, and were this spectacularly unsuccessful in getting things done, how long do you think they would survive in the real world? Yet the Department of Energy has thrived and grown as a bureaucracy for 33 years, and there are no signs of it ever being called to task.

5. The Community Reinvestment Act of 1977 was passed because of the publicity achieved by activist groups alleging that banks discriminated against minorities by denying them home loans. Studies made by the activist groups documented higher rates of loan denial to

minorities and demanded corrective action. Of course, amidst all the negative press, one fact tended to be overlooked: that banks rejected minority applications not because of racism, but because the income-to-debt ratios of minorities tended to fall below the ratios used by banks for all applicants. No matter, the federal government felt compelled to correct the perceived wrong.

In the years following, activist groups, notable among them ACORN, used the law to pressure and threaten banks to increase "affordable housing" loans to minorities regardless of the increased financial risk to the banks. Banks began accepting the loan losses as a cost of doing business. In the 1990's, HUD and Congress began pressuring Fannie Mae and Freddie Mac to lower their lending standards to make affordable housing available to even more citizens. These two semi-governmental institutions, since their inception, were designed to provide stability in the mortgage market by purchasing home loans that met their standards. The standards were in place to offer a reasonable guarantee that the borrower would be able to repay the loan. As the standards were lowered, the riskiness of the loans they purchased increased. These are the now-infamous subprime mortgages.

For twenty years, Freddie and Fannie's lowered standards fueled increased demand for housing and thus an exponential increase in home values. (The Federal Reserve Bank encouraged the bubble by keeping interest rates extremely low by historical standards.) As Fannie and Freddie lowered standards, banks and mortgage brokers, driven by potential profits, jumped into the subprime fracas by providing more "creative" loan products, accepting no down payments, not requiring proof of income, offering interest-only mortgages, and thereby substantially increasing the systemic risk.

Simultaneously, Fannie and Freddie began to "securitize" the loans -- package them as a financial product and then sell shares to investors. This allowed immediate realization of huge cash profits, rather than waiting on the traditional long-term recovery of investment as the mortgages are repaid over time. Most of the investors bought the packaged loan securities with the false assumption that the mortgage-based products underlying the shares held low risk, because mortgages were traditionally the most conservative and secure types of loans. Other financial institutions began to offer the same securitized products. The sums of money involved were enormous....the inherent risks were a ticking time bomb pervading our entire financial system.[104]

Beginning in 2001, the Bush Administration warned of systemic risk in the Fannie and Freddie balance sheets, and called for increased regulatory oversight. These warnings continued through 2006, the last attempt being a Senate bill authored by Sen. John McCain. House and Senate Democrats, led by Rep. Barney Frank and Sen. Charles Schumer, blocked every effort at regulatory restraint, calling the agencies "fundamentally sound" and praising their record of funding housing for the poor and minorities.[105] Ironically, in a situation where restrictive and recuperative regulation was truly needed, Democrat legislators, who routinely cry for increased regulation of our free market system, not only failed to act, but prevented action.

Unfortunately, we as a nation are all too familiar with the consequences. In 2007, the sub-prime mortgage crisis began as borrowers missed payments and lenders were forced to foreclose. As foreclosures mounted, the enormous risks inherent in the balance sheets of all financial institutions were exposed. Ultimately, this triggered the massive financial meltdown, bank failures and Great Recession of 2008. Fannie and Freddie are now in receivership (i.e., bankrupt) and are propped up by hundreds of billions of federal bail-out dollars, and an unlimited line of credit from the U.S. Government. A speculative worst-case scenario puts the cost to taxpayers at One Trillion dollars[106]! Millions of Americans lost and are still losing their homes and/or their jobs. We haven't seen the end of it. In October 2009, unemployment reached 10.2%, the highest rate in 26 years, and as of this writing, neither unemployment nor housing have begun a substantial recovery.

Since Congress just passed the 2010 Financial Reform legislation, it is prudent to remember the rule of long-term unintended consequences.

6. Entitlements and their destructive, addictive effects were discussed above, but not in the context of government failure. Medicare, enacted in 1965, cost a mere $3 Billion in1966, its initial year of implementation. In 1967, the House Ways and Means Committee projected it would cost $12 Billion by 1990. The actual cost of Medicare in 1990 was $110 Billion. In other words, it cost ten times more than originally estimated[107]. In 2009, the total cost of Medicare was $512 Billion, and grows every year. In 2008, Medicare costs exceeded taxes collected for the first time. It is projected to be completely insolvent by 2017[108].

The graph below is a stunning visual depiction of the historical and projected growth of Medicare spending, as a percentage of Gross Domestic Product[109]. The dark line is

Medicare including Parts A, B and D. (The gray line is Social Security Old Age, Survivors and Disability) Medicare has increased, and will continue to grow exponentially, with devastating economic impact.

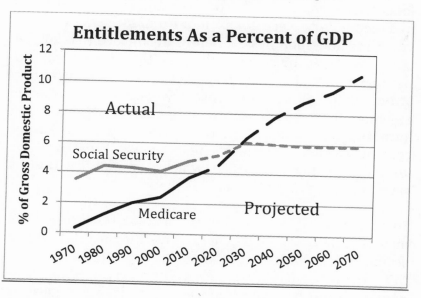

Disregarding Medicare's projected insolvency, the Bush II administration, and the 2003 Republican Congress, enacted even more addictive entitlements in the form of the Medicare Prescription Drug Benefit. This further increased our deficit spending and hastened the "day of reckoning" for Medicare.

Now, of course, there is Obamacare. Our populace has been promised by the Democrats that this legislative abomination, which has been estimated to *cost* $940 Billion over ten years will actually *decrease* our national deficit.[110] Would you 'bet a paycheck' on the accuracy of their financial projections? That was a terrible pun, by the way. Every American is involuntarily betting all of their future paychecks on the outcome.

Furthermore....

Even those functions that Conservatives and Constitutionalists agree are legitimate functions of the federal government -- border control, national security and the military -- are not exempt from this general rule of governmental ineptness. Before reading the following commentary, it must be emphasized that the authors are not questioning the need for effective border control or a strong military. On the contrary, both are absolutely essential to the survival of our country. Nor are the authors questioning the patriotism and loyalty of border control agents or military personnel. What will be discussed is the manner in which our political leaders carry out these constitutional mandates.

So much has been recently written concerning the miserable failure of our federal government to provide a secure border with Mexico, that it is superfluous to detail this circumstance in these pages. For political reasons, our national leaders have ignored what is essentially an invasion of millions of illegal immigrants across our southern border. While providing low-cost, unskilled and semi-skilled labor, they take advantage of the social programs in our country, and substantially increase the cost of health care, education, welfare and criminal justice.[111] Moreover, we are becoming a bilingual country by default[112]. The solutions to stop illegal immigration are incredibly straightforward. The overwhelming majority of U.S. citizens insist that our borders be sovereign, yet our federal government appears to be powerless to do anything effective.

Our country maintains what is unarguably the most powerful fighting force on the planet. Our nation has a superb fighting cadre of brave patriotic individuals.

However, the governmental / political application of U.S. military force is rife with mistakes, and is often plagued by misunderstanding or underestimation of the enemy by our political leaders. This applies to both Democrat and Republican administrations.

For example, prior to the start of the Civil War in April 1861, the politicians on both sides thought the war would require but a few months of gallant service to defeat the other side. Both Union and Confederate political leaders thought it would be a brief but "glorious" conflict on the field of honor. The reality was horribly different. Emerging weapons technology far outstripped the battlefield tactics of the day, resulting in tremendous human carnage – over 600,000 Americans killed in four years of fighting. The Union commanding generals in the East, until Lincoln promoted Grant, were incredibly inept, self-serving or just cowardly, and cost the U.S. Army thousands of lives, and very nearly lost the war. The ultimate savagery and loss of life of the war, in part, induced the victorious Union to impose the punishment of Reconstruction on the South, and delayed true reunification for years.[113]

Vietnam. For the Boomers reading this, no further elaboration is necessary. For those younger readers, the Vietnam war was a 13 year tragedy expending 58,000 American lives, 304,000 American casualties[114], between two and three million Vietnamese lives, and $170 billion U.S. taxpayer dollars (in 1970 dollars -- roughly $686 Billion in 2008 dollars[115]). It began in the late 1950's and early 1960's as a force of advisers and trainers aimed at supporting a fledging democratic (though highly corrupt) South Vietnamese government against Communist infiltration. Lyndon Johnson and his advisers used a minor 1964 incident in the Tonkin Gulf to bully Congress into a massive escalation of U.S. involvement. By 1965, U.S. troops had begun directly waging the war. Although U.S. forces achieved complete tactical victory in the field, our military was hamstrung by political second-guessing and restrictions. Also, we did not truly grasp how to strategically fight a counter-insurgency until late in the war.[116] After years of watching our sons and daughters sent to this seemingly never-ending grinder, our nation lost the heart and the political will to continue the fight. Congress refused to support the South Vietnamese government after our troops left following the 1973 Truce, and essentially acquiesced to the 1975 North Vietnamese invasion and ultimate victory. The obscene cost of the war accomplished virtually nothing of strategic benefit for America. What it did quite effectively was literally tear our country apart and, for years thereafter, destroy our national will and optimism. More crucially, it spawned the seeds of activist liberalism that ultimately morphed into today's generation of Neo-totalitarians.

As recently as the 2003 War in Iraq, George W. Bush and his advisors ignored the warning that his father had heeded in the first Gulf War – that deposing Saddam Hussein would unleash internecine bloodshed and potential civil war. It did, and only large scale expenditures of American lives and dollars have begun to correct the mistake. As 2010 comes to a close, even though the threat of civil war has diminished, and most of our troops have left the country, the future of Iraq as an emerging "democracy" is fragile and cloudy. Politically, this war again divided the nation, and was a proximate cause of Democrat victories in 2006 and 2008. As these Democrats now rush headlong toward totalitarianism, it can be argued that the so-called "Bush Doctrine" has provided Iraq with a hope for democracy but at the unwitting cost of American democracy. Moreover, this lack of principled decision-making in the use of force will undoubtedly infect us with political timidness in confronting the growing threat of a nuclear Iran.

The foregoing is not intended to denigrate the sacrifice and bravery of those serving in the military. Our warriors are the true and ultimate patriots. We are a grateful nation who celebrate their dedication to preserving our freedom and way of life. Nor is it an argument to discourage us from maintaining a strong national defense. On the contrary, as stated above, this is one of the few functions that should be performed by the federal government, and given the aggressive (and often evil) nature of mankind, is absolutely essential, as it clearly was in World War II.

Our argument is presented to reinforce the position that government is just not the best way to get something done. Sometimes, as in the case of national defense, it is the only feasible way, but it is almost never a good way. We seek only to demonstrate the fallacy of paternalistic totalitarianism. We desire to underscore our Founders' belief that the role of our federal government should be a very limited role.

In fairness, our discussion should conclude with this: Government can accomplish good and prevent evil when focused and targeted to an essential mission. For example, the FBI is the premier law enforcement agency in the world, and does a superb job of tracking and arresting lawbreakers. The Centers for Disease Control works to increase public safety and prevent epidemics in our country and around the world. Federal and state prosecutors attack and defeat the cruelty of organized crime. The key to effective governance, as our Founders clearly grasped, was focusing and limiting its scope and power.

The Parable of California

As California Goes, So Goes The Nation. This was once a tribute to the trendiness of Californians in terms of fashion, entertainment, and social experimentation in general. Now, it predicts a very uncertain national future. California is dealing with the consequences of two decades of exponential state government spending increases, "progressive" state tax policies, liberal social welfare programs, pro-union anti-business regulation, a surge of illegal immigration, and increasingly intrusive environmentalism.

California, it would seem, is a real-life laboratory for studying the progressive policies that are envisioned for the nation by the current administration. The question, then, is what does this portend for America? Read on......

California tax statistics, as of 2010:
- It has the second highest state income tax rate in the country (8.25% over $37,000, 9.6% over $47,000).[117] Only Oregon's is higher.
- It has the highest state sales tax rate in the country (8.25%). It is one of only seven states that apply general sales tax to gasoline purchases.[118]
- It has the third highest state gasoline tax (35.3 cents per gallon)[119]

All this taxing is necessary to fund the highest level of state government spending in the country ($365 billion per year) and the fourth largest per capita state spending ($10,106)[120]. California's spending growth has far outpaced inflation and its population growth. According to columnist George Will, if state spending increases, since 1990, had been limited to inflation and population growth percentages, the state would now have a $15 Billion surplus, instead of the massive deficits described below.[121]

An example of California's spending philosophy is their Medicaid program, Medi-Cal, which is the nation's largest state program and one of the most generous in the country. It covers 6.8 million or about 17% of the state's population, including one third of the children in the state. It pays for 46% of the births in California. It consumes 19% of the state budget. It provides such extras as home health care, hospice care, hearing aids and certain drugs not covered under Medicare Part D. Until recently, it covered dental and optometric care. It even provides "restricted" medical services such as emergency care and pregnancy/childbirth care to illegal immigrants.[122]

Unfortunately, the state's high tax rate was insufficient to prevent a $42 billion budget deficit in 2009, as the economy slowed in 2007 and 2008 and tax revenue fell.[123] Theoretically, the state mandates balanced budgets. Even though it recently raised taxes and cut spending, it still projects a $20 billion deficit in Fiscal Year 2010.

The California state government is essentially bankrupt. In July 2009, the state was paying debts with $2.6 billion worth of I.O.U.s.[124] Very bad news. In November, the state resorted to confiscating an additional 10% in withholding of state income taxes from workers' paychecks to inject cash into state coffers.[125]

Facing massive budget shortfalls, the state legislature's response, in February 2009, included a $12.8 billion increase in state income, sales and vehicle taxes. California is now competing with New York to see who can tax their citizens into oblivion. However, in May 2009, California voters soundly rejected five of six ballot measures designed to prevent insolvency through tax increases.[126] Accurately reading the mood of the electorate, Governor Schwarzenegger vowed not to further increase taxes and has undertaken or proposed fairly drastic reductions in state funding of public schools and universities, Medi-Cal, state workers' salaries, and lastly the prison system. It must be a comforting thought to Californians that their penal system has begun the early release of over 6,000 inmates to cut costs.[127]

Since business is the catalyst for any economic revival, a rebound may be tough. California is not kind to business. According to the Tax Foundation, it has the fourth highest corporate income tax rate in America (8.84% on the first dollar earned), and was rated 48th on its 2010 Business Tax Climate Index.[128] Business regulation is heavier than other states. For example, California is one of only four states that requires overtime be paid on a daily basis rather than weekly, and has enacted a minimum wage of $8 per hour, significantly higher than the federal minimum wage. California mandates lunch breaks for part time workers. These rules increase labor costs and put California businesses at a disadvantage. The Golden State is not a right-to-work state; employees are forced to join unions in the workplace. California requires licenses or special credentials for an amazing 177 unique occupations, thus impeding competition. The state is ranked 37th worst for workers compensation costs. CNBC has rated California as the third most expensive state for businesses. Forbes magazine rates it 40th in its annual report on the best states for business.[129]

It is no coincidence that California had the third highest unemployment rate of any state, 12.4% in May 2010, exceeded only by Nevada and Michigan[130] -- and thus had the highest number of home foreclosures in the nation --

over 72,000 in May 2010 alone -- a trend which began in 2007 when over one half million California families lost their homes to foreclosure.[131] California's working folks have ultimately paid the price for their state government's regulatory heavy-handedness.

Deciding to lead the fight against "global warming", California is the lone state to regulate carbon dioxide emissions of both vehicles and stationary sources.[132] Cost estimates of this regulation to state consumers and businesses vary wildly, some as high as $500 billion over 30 years. Dangerously, no one really knows what the total costs may be. One thing is certain: car buyers and energy consumers will pay significantly more than they do now. For example, even the lowest cost estimates for vehicle CO_2 emission controls (by the California Air Resources Board staff) are over $1000 per car by 2016. At 1.5 million vehicles sold per year in the state, that regulation will cost CA consumers $1.5 Billion per year. Car manufacturers put the cost per vehicle at over $3000, *tripling* the outlay by consumers. Nearly every expert admits this effort will only reduce CO_2 emissions by 0.5%, and will have no impact whatsoever on "climate change". This conclusion applies not only to California but to the entire nation.

In a another effort to change the globe's climate, a 2008 executive order increased the percentage of California electricity that must be obtained from renewable sources (wind, solar, geothermal, biomass, etc.) to 33% by 2021. The state Public Utilities Commission forecasts a Kilowatt Hour price increase of 28% to pay for additional generation and transmission facilities -- this on top of what are already some of the highest electricity rates in the country.[133] Reliable and reasonably priced electricity is a cornerstone of economic stability and growth. Somewhere along the way, California forgot about this fact.

California's education system has not had great success, which is a grim harbinger of the state's, and by projection, our nation's economic future. In 2009 standardized math and reading scores from fourth grade and eighth grade, California students ranked 47th, 48th or 49th in the nation.[134]   Interestingly, according to the National Education Association, California's unionized teachers are the most highly paid in the nation.[135] (Although the state's per pupil expenditures are very close to the national average.[136])

Pinpointing the cause of such dismal results is not easy. However, a factor cited in research indicates that demographics play a role in student performance.[137]   In 2009, 49% of the student population was Hispanic. Fully 21% of the student population (over one million children) were classified as *English Learners in Spanish*, requiring special teachers, classes and resources.   Over 209,000 California teachers were providing either primary language instruction or supplemental instruction.[138]

Consider this anecdote which is symbolic of the state's educational quandary: Ricky Nelson and the character he played in that quintessential idealization of [1950's] suburbia, *The Adventures of Ozzie and Harriet*, attended Hollywood High, a school that is now 75 percent Hispanic and that the New York Times accurately described in 2003 as "a typically overcrowded, vandalism-prone urban campus".[139]

What is the bottom line? California ranks 49th in net migration loss, i.e., there were more people leaving the state than moving in. This is amazing considering the huge influx of immigrants coming into the state. (Approximately 2.8 million immigrants are in CA illegally, or *8% of the total state population.* [140]) In the decade of 1999-2008, the net migration loss was 1.4 million people. According to economists Laffer and Moore, the ex-Californians are the *"highest achievers and those with the most wealth, capital and entrepreneurial drive".*[141] That is, those who are most likely to invest, create jobs and pay taxes.

This is all happening in a state that is absolutely blessed with one of the world's best climates and most spectacular natural beauty. It is a shame that such misguided government meddling has ruined California's image as the Mecca of America.

So what? Why should we care about California?

Simply this: The current Administration and Democrats in Congress want to essentially mirror what California has done. They have either enacted, proposed, or are considering very similar federal efforts in terms of increased social, health and educational programs, pro-union legislation, business regulation, immigration changes, energy intervention, etc. From the California experience, we now know these actions will result in the same exponential spending increases, tax increases, and economic turmoil that have afflicted California citizens and businesses.

Finally, as in California, there is a risk that the "movers and shakers", the entrepreneurs and investors, will be robbed of any incentives and driven away. If you are an achiever, if you have any work ethic or entrepreneurial spirit, or even a desire to be personally responsible for your own life, to where will you emigrate if America becomes California?

Part Four:
Restoring Our Values and Saving America

My God! How little do my countrymen know what precious blessings they are in possession of, and which no other people on earth enjoy! --- Thomas Jefferson

The Generation That Saved America

"Millennials" is a popular term used to describe the generation of Americans born between 1980 and 2000. At the time of this writing, they are under 30 years old. This group of young patriots will unquestionably determine what America is to become for many generations. It is for this reason that Conservatives of all ages should reach out to our young folks. *This must be Job One*

Are we destined to become the America suggested in the opening story of the *Summer Vacation*? Or will we restore America to the patriotic values and freedoms of our Founders? It is the Millennials who will ultimately provide the answer to these questions.

This generation, over 80 million strong, has already begun to shape national policy. The Democratic sweep of Congress and the Presidency in 2008 was due in large measure to the voting preferences of the "under-30" age demographic. Millennials voted for Obama by a two to one margin. At this point, only about half are old enough to vote, but two-thirds of those identify themselves as Democrats. By 2020, Millennials will comprise 36% of the electorate, and will dominate the political agenda of America.[142]

Research indicates that Millennials are more ethnically and racially diverse, and are more tolerant and accepting of this fact than older generations. They are certainly more technologically savvy, indeed, electronics play a key role in their communications and social life. They are less assertive in matters of national security, but are more supportive of a progressive domestic agenda. They value "working and playing well with others" but do not put a high work ethic at the top of their agenda.[143]

If Millennials continue to vote for the "progressive" agenda in the next two national elections, the country's shift toward totalitarianism will increase exponentially and become virtually irreversible. The question must be asked: Was this generation taught to embrace freedom and traditional American values? The evidence of recent elections suggests that they may not. The generation of Baby Boomers may have failed their children in this regard. Boomers too often have allowed television and pop-culture to set the agenda and teach values. Sesame Street and MTV ruled back then, but Jon Stewart, Bill Maher and Stephen Colbert are the influence now.

Time and experience will ultimately change the outlook of many Millennials. Becoming   productive tax-paying citizens who try to provide for their families and increase their standard of living usually is sufficient to encourage moderation and conservatism.   However, and this is crucial, we as a nation do not have the luxury of time to let this maturation process occur. Two Obama terms coupled with 10 years of a Democrat super majority in Congress will produce entitlement programs, deficits, increased taxes, Supreme Court appointments, immigration reform, etc., that will lock the U.S. into totalitarianism and fiscal despair for generations, if not forever.

The following are imperatives for the survival of Conservatism, and the future of our nation:

- Conservatives MUST appeal to Millennial core beliefs. If the Republican Party is to survive, it must recruit and field candidates at every level who relate to (and are close in age to) Millennials. Millennials must be brought into Party leadership positions and policy decisions immediately.

- Conservatives MUST embrace electronic tools and the internet to reach those under 30.   The Millennials expect rapid-fire updates and instantaneous feedback, and Conservatives had better employ an electronic haven of *avant-garde* resources to attract them. Facebook, You Tube, LinkedIn and Twitter have to be key communication tools for Conservatives at both the state and federal level. Blogs and email messages are crucial to presenting the message, but in a way that will be widely accessed and read. The Republican Party should hire Millennial communication consultants to help all of us become fully engaged.

- Conservatives MUST reach out to churches that are popular with Millennials. Church leaders should be encouraged to teach about our nation's patriotic values and religious legacy, in addition to redemption.

- Conservatives MUST become more involved in State Boards of Regents to influence college curricula and encourage diversity of political thought among college faculty.

- Conservatives MUST become involved in local school boards and be aggressive in choosing textbooks. It is imperative that Conservatives challenge and discourage textbooks that cast historical actions in terms of today's political correctness, that encourage "progressive" ideas, that chastise America for failures rather than celebrating success, or that minimize or disparage American values.

Freedom is never more than one generation away from extinction. We didn't pass it to our children in the bloodstream. It must be fought for, protected, and handed on for them to do the same.
--- President Ronald Reagan

Strategies and Goals Must Precede Action

To save our nation, there must be a revolution of action by our loyal citizens, action that is well thought out, planned and executed; all within the context of existing political rights, naturally...while they still exist, and while there is still time. The base is in place. It is fed up, but it is fired up. Tea Parties and Town Hall Meetings have proven that the fuse has been lit. But much more is needed. Conservatives are crying out for principled leadership.

Leadership of Conservative organizations and political parties must define the types of politico-citizens in the U.S., understand the motivation of each, and devise appropriate strategies and messages which convey the urgency of the threats to our nation, appeal to their patriotism and love of country, and convince each type to embrace the beliefs necessary to affect change. Or marginalize and defeat those who cannot be reached.

The essential types of politico-citizens in the United States in 2010:

- Neo-totalitarians (Leftists, Statists, Socialists or Progressives),
- Conservatives (Libertarians or Constitutionalists),
- Independents (or the "Center Right")
- The Politically Uninformed
- The Dependent Class (a growing fifth cadre and subservient subset of the Neo-totalitarians, deriving some or all of its subsistence from government, and eagerly voting to preserve and increase the handouts.)

Know Your Political Enemy and Fight Back

The struggle may be a moral one or it may be a physical one, and it may be both moral and physical, but it must be a struggle. Power concedes nothing without a demand. It never did and it never will. Find out just what any people will quietly submit to and you have found out the exact measure of injustice and wrong which will be imposed upon them, and these will continue till they are resisted with either words or blows, or with both. The limits of tyrants are prescribed by the endurance of those who they oppress.
--- Frederick Douglass, Abolitionist and Freedom Fighter

Who are the Neo-totalitarians? They are Democrat politicians who desire more dependent constituencies to maintain and increase their power. They are far left organizations and their funding sources (the most prominent being George Soros and, incredibly, the U.S. Government). They are "civil libertarians" who perversely fight for a stronger and more controlling state, all to the detriment of liberty. They are Community Organizers who unleash legions of paid grass-root operatives in the ACORN model. They are Labor Union leadership who broker political support for legal leverage even though rank and file union members are unaware they are economically supporting Neo-totalitarianism. And lastly, the so-called "Mainstream Media", which has become the promoter and the defender of the Neo-totalitarian agenda

The examples above describe the most dangerous aspect of the Neo-totalitarian movement - the Power Manipulators. In responding to the Power Manipulators and their organizations, Conservatives must face the reality that we are in a literal war for our country. Regardless of what their public rhetoric may claim, Neo-totalitarian Power Manipulators will never respond to overtures of bi-partisanship, compromise or appeals to patriotism and values. Regardless of what their motivation may be, their goal is elitist-controlled totalitarianism. They will not be swayed by argument nor deterred by short-term setbacks. They can only be defeated. They must be defeated politically, of course, but they also must be defeated in the hearts of our countrymen. It will be a daunting task.

This is not conspiracy theory. Go to some of the following websites and read their stated goals: the American Civil Liberties Union, MoveOn.org, People for the American Way, Center for American Progress, Association of Community Organizations for Reform Now (ACORN), Americans United for the Separation of Church and State, Greenpeace, Media Matters, Democratic Energy, Gay and Lesbian Alliance Against Defamation, Act Now to Stop War and End Racism (ANSWER) -- the list goes on.

Conservative organizations and political parties must employ tough, hard-ball tactics that match our adversaries. Saul Alinsky's 1971 text, *Rules for Radicals*, which the Neo-totalitarians have employed as a tactical manual for decades, should be studied not just to understand and defend against Leftist tactics, but to use as a primer against them. It cannot be over-emphasized that we are in a war for our country.

Alinsky was a dedicated Marxist organizer and activist who learned his craft in the Depression Era, and was committed to deconstructing our capitalist system, empowering the "Have-Nots" by confiscating wealth from the "Haves". *Rules for Radicals* was written as an instruction manual for the young radicals of the 1970's. He advocated gradual transition of power by infiltrating the power system, and organizing the masses (whether a company, a community or a nation) to advocate for change. Consider the following Alinsky quotes, and compare to how the left wing of the Democrat Party, and in particular the Barack Obama inner circle, have approached power. As you read these quotes, think about, for example, the bold lies told concerning the financial impact of health care reform. Think about the relentless ridicule of Sarah Palin. Think about how many times Democrats have appealed to the "middle class". Alinsky wrote[144]:

- "There's another reason for working inside the system. Dostoevsky said that taking a new step is what people fear most. Any revolutionary change must be preceded by a passive, affirmative, non-challenging attitude toward change among the mass of our people. They must feel so frustrated, so defeated, so lost, so futureless in the prevailing system that they are willing to let go of the past and change the future. This acceptance is the reformation essential to any revolution."

- "To bring on this reformation requires that the organizer work inside the system, among not only the middle class, but the 40 per cent of American families – more than seventy million people – whose income range from $5,000 to $10,000 a year [in 1971, i.e. the working class]. "

- "Whenever we think about social change, the question of means and ends arises. The man of action views the issue of means and ends in pragmatic and strategic terms. He has no other problem; he thinks only of his actual resources and the possibilities of various choices of action. He asks of *ends* only whether they are achievable and worth

the cost; of *means*, only whether they will work. ...
The real arena is corrupt and bloody."

- "The tenth rule... is you do what you can with what
  you have and clothe it with moral garments...."

- "Ridicule is man's most potent weapon."

- "Pick the target, freeze it, personalize it, and
  polarize it. Whenever possible, go outside the
  expertise of the enemy. Look for ways to increase
  insecurity, anxiety and uncertainty... Don't try to
  attack abstract corporations or bureaucracies.
  Identify a responsible individual. "

I would imagine that Conservatives reading the above
philosophies will immediately recognize the deceit,
duplicity, lack of honor and absence of integrity implicit in
Alinsky's tactics.   Again, I remind my readers that
Conservatives are in a war and we are losing. In fact, with
the exceptions of the Reagan Administration and the 1994
Republican Congressional victory, Conservatives have
been losing for 75 years.

A wonderful example of how Conservatives can employ
Alinsky-style tactics is the September 2009 undercover
sting of ACORN, conducted by the Conservative group
BigGovernment.com. and initially brought to the public via
Fox News. Videos of ACORN Housing employees helping a
pimp to defraud loan institutions (and taxpayers) led to
the Senate vote to stop federal ACORN funding and ending
the Census Bureau plan to use ACORN operatives to
conduct the 2010 census. Some ACORN affiliates are
changing their name and laying low, but they will emerge
again. Conservatives must be constantly vigilant.

Sarah Palin, former Governor of Alaska, reached national prominence as a common-sense Conservative and Republican candidate for Vice-President in the 2008 election. Not only did the leftist media target her for condescension and ridicule, but the Left, in general, mounted a determined attack through constant multiple ethics complaints. These complaints, in her case, proved groundless. All such attacks must be defended, but they are expensive and force the target to redirect time and energy from Conservative action, to dealing with frivolous and unsubstantiated charges. It is a brilliant, albeit completely unethical, political tactic. As unpalatable as the tactic may be, I believe that Conservative groups must consider employing similar strategies simply to level the field and lay bare the deceit of the Neo-totalitarians.

Our judicial system, particularly at the federal level where judges are appointed and are virtually unaccountable to the people, have proven to be the battleground of choice for Neo-totalitarian Power Manipulators. The ruling of an activist judge can achieve a far-reaching "progressive" impact at minimal cost. Conservatives must become assertive in this battleground.

Conservatives must create and fund a legal arm that, for lack of a better name, could be called the "Anti-ACLU". There are already private groups that field legal teams and challenge issues on a piecemeal basis, but I envision a large, high-profile, nationally recognized entity that will not only counter the Neo-totalitarian based lawsuits, but will proactively and aggressively sue to maintain American values on all fronts. This group could be an "umbrella" for many others that are already in the fray, providing funding and setting a prioritized agenda. The Heritage Foundation would be an excellent home for such an entity, and in 2010 has even begun *Heritage Action for America*, a 501(c)4 tax-exempt organization formed to influence Congress directly.

Going beyond the Power Manipulators, there are two sub-manifestations of Neo-totalitarians: True Believers and Trendy Followers. True Believers derive their beliefs from linking their emotion-laden politics to the very heart of their self-worth as a person. They are what they believe. If you question these beliefs, you question their personal self-worth, and they respond viciously. Arguments based in logic, or sound financial or economic reality, will fall on deaf ears. Realistically, they must be marginalized; for they will probably always object to patriotic values and fiscal prudence. True Believers are smugly convinced they are the hope.

Our time has come, our movement is real, and change is coming to America. We are the ones we've been waiting for. We are the change that we seek.
--- Senator Obama on Super Tuesday 2008

Marginalization may indeed be the easiest tactic. Recent Gallup surveys in every state have shown that 42% of respondents identify themselves as "Conservative". Only 20% consider themselves as "Liberal", with 35% being "Moderate".[145] It is probable that only a small minority of this 20% are the True Believers. Most fall into the next category -- Trendy Followers.

Whereas Power Manipulators must be defeated and True Believers must be marginalized, Trendy Liberal Followers are another story. There is a probability that they can be reached because ultimately they follow others who determine what is fashionable. As Conservative momentum accelerates and Conservative Republicans begin winning elections at all levels, human nature will entice Trendy Liberal Followers to switch trends. It's simple -- Patriotism is sexy -- don't be left out.

Environmental extremism and "global warming" provide us with a prime example to study Neo-totalitarians in action.

- Power Manipulators (the United Nations IPCC, Greenpeace, Moveon.org, Al Gore's Alliance for Climate Protection and RePowerAmerica.org) use the "cause" to promote increased government intervention, more taxes and more wealth transfers from individuals to government. Moreover, the Manipulators act as "advisors" on the wealth transfer, or surreptitiously invest in soon-to-be-heavily subsidized "green" endeavors.
- The True Believers, in turn, conjure scientific pseudo-evidence through the use of computer climate models and "cherry-picked" tree-ring temperature measurements, etc.
- Finally, Trendy Followers, in this case the media outlets, distribute every sighting of warming "evidence" as a catastrophe, and hype the "crisis" with "Green" Hollywood actors, who lend their questionable scientific expertise to the fable.

It all ends in our living rooms, where the average citizen, who doesn't want to be left out of "saving the planet", swallows every single regulation, law and tax hike with gullible acceptance.

How to Influence the Media in Reestablishing American Principles

Fox News thrives, while NBC, CBS, ABC, PBS, MSNBC and CNN all wither. During the October 2009 ratings, Fox News primetime had more viewers than CNN, HLN and

MSNBC combined. In the first three months of 2010, according to Neilson, CNN's primetime viewers decreased by 42%, yet they laughably maintain they are the only network delivering "unbiased" news.[146] The Wall Street Journal increases readership while The New York Times is bankrupt and other newspapers' circulation declines by 11% in 2009 and 9% in 2010.[147]

Americans thirst for a media that tells the truth and reinforces the values they treasure. Yet the "mainstream" media outlets continue to distort the news, propagandize the "progressive" agenda, and attempt to demean and criticize those who disagree with their views. It is evident that the ideology of the liberal elite who control these media outlets outweighs the economic price they are paying.

A recent Pew Research Center study found that only 26% of Americans believe that news organizations are not politically biased.[148] Bernard Goldberg, a respected CBS, HBO and FOX journalist for years, has written extensively on the bias and hypocrisy of what he refers to as the "lamestream" media.

NBC (and its corporate parent, General Electric) has placed its bets with the Neo-totalitarians, and does everything in its electronic power to ignore or belittle Conservatives. CBS News, in its zeal to attack the previous Republican Administration, allowed its flagship anchor Dan Rather to report unverified facts to smear President Bush. (Ultimately, this liberal zeal cost Rather his job.) PBS follows its proud liberal tradition as its audience disappears. CNN still clings to Ted Turner's elitist one-world ideology, and literally insults Conservative America during their coverage of Tea Party events. The former so-called "Mainstream Media" is anything but.

A very recent example is the Immigration Law passed in Arizona in April 2010. For weeks leading up to its passage, and especially just after the Arizona governor signed it, the national media almost exclusively focused on the opposition. Viewers, listeners and readers were exposed to countless stories of nationwide protests, lawsuits threatened or filed, boycotts of Arizona products, and pundits comparing Arizona to Nazi Germany. What you did not see or hear was any report of the vast majority of Arizona citizens (and indeed American citizens) who adamantly support any level of government trying to protect our borders against illegal entry.[149]

The ongoing transition of viewership and readership away from liberal media outlets toward those that are more traditional, unbiased and/or conservative has not convinced their executives and boards to alter their editorial bias. It is therefore time for Conservatives to initiate more direct action against the propagandists. Two possible actions come to mind.

First, conservative groups (not affiliated with the Republican Party) should consider boycott tactics that proved devastatingly effective in the Civil Rights era. Consider orchestrating national letter writing and emailing campaigns directly to mainstream media advertisers notifying them that their products and services will be boycotted. Explain to them the reason is that they support a media that no longer exemplifies journalistic integrity or American values.

And then do it – carry out the boycott. Select a few very high-profile advertisers and target the boycott to their products or services. Of course, the liberal media will condemn and vilify the action. Individuals in isolation have virtually no influence on the corporate executives who set the tone for these outlets, but Boards of Directors who see advertising revenues diminish hopefully will act in the best interest of their corporations.

Secondly, Conservatives must be innovative in using the internet to bypass these media, especially when communicating with the "totally connected" Millennials. We must urge conservative entrepreneurs to create conservative-toned social networking sites, career sites, singles sites, and charitable sites. Blogs and email distribution lists are effective tools to bring a message quickly, widely, and comprehensively.

The Dependent Class: Weaning Our People From Creeping Dependent Mentality

Fight against progressive taxation and fight for a flat tax or Fair Tax. Until every citizen of this country is required to help pay the tab, however modest their contribution may be, it will be impossible to inspire or motivate them to leave the womb-like addictive embrace of their entitlements. A system that allows half of our citizens to not pay income taxes is a system that is inherently unfair, and will ultimately feed class warfare and destroy economic motivation. Changing our tax system will be the battle of our generation. But it must be fought if we are to preserve America. If it is not changed within a very few years, the dependent voters will outnumber taxpaying voters, and then it will be too late to vote at all.

Fundamental tax code changes will not happen easily or quickly, but we must start. Perhaps a first "baby step" would be the elimination of Child Tax Credits and Earned Income Tax Credits, which are nothing but hidden welfare payments. Ultimately, it will take determined, consistent and unrelenting leadership from a revitalized and empowered Republican Party to enact a fairer tax code.

Additionally, we must transform the entitlements. As discussed, they are addictive, morally destructive, and fiscally unsustainable. They punish self-sufficiency and reward dependency. Again, more details on a plan are provided in a later section.

Overcoming Racial Politics: How to Reverse the Tide of Political Victimhood

It's not about race, it's about truth. Blacks are patriots.... Hispanics are patriots.... Asians are patriots. Notice that there was not one ethnic "hyphen-American" used in the preceding sentence. Hyphens divide us nationally just as they do grammatically. All one has to do is observe the ethnicity of our military to demonstrate that patriotism crosses all racial lines.

The American Dream, inspired by American Values, lives for every race and culture. Certainly there is racism, it has always existed and always will. The Biblical parable of the Good Samaritan was predicated on racism. Jews in the time of Jesus reviled the Samaritan race, yet a Samaritan helped a Jewish man attacked and beaten by robbers. Humans are imperfect and are subject to a variety of sins – racism is but one. However, constant claims of victimhood and demands for political spoils do nothing to end racism and, conversely, contribute to resentment of the race or culture claiming the reparations, and divide us as a nation.

Moreover, the political spoils handed out by politicians create dependency, not self- sufficiency. Neo-totalitarian politicians desire a growing block of dependent voters, and they care not if it takes racial strife or sociological damage to the dependents, to achieve it. Ever-expanding government hand-outs create an insidious form of slavery, the dependency of individuals locked into artificially compartmentalized boundaries, who become servile pawns to a "benevolent" government. If an end to racism and betterment of a minority group are the goals, Neo-totalitarianism is not the roadmap.

It is an undeniable fact that, in the history of our country, black citizens were mistreated. Segregation and discrimination existed, and may still occur surreptitiously in corrupt and evil environments. However, these wrongs have been overwhelmingly righted. Equal Opportunity laws at all levels prevent them. Billions of dollars have been and are still being spent on affirmative action programs, diversity programs, set-asides, contract quotas, head-start programs, Title I education programs, *No Child Left Behind* programs, minority-based college scholarships, etc. Educational and entrepreneurial opportunities have essentially been equalized in this country. The American Dream can be seized by every American, regardless of their race. Every race in America has its millionaires, and every race has its homeless. Is America perfect – no, but it never will be. Don't wait on it.

Most American citizens oppose illegal immigration, not just by Hispanics, but by any ethnicity. Americans want everyone in this country to play by the rules and pay their fair share of taxes. Americans resent having to fund a huge enforcement effort to protect our border from invasion. They also oppose "solving" the "immigration problem" by granting amnesty to millions who violated, and continue to flaunt our laws. Immigration advocacy groups, the Neo-totalitarians and the media try desperately to portray this as racism. It is not.

Immigration is a legal and economic issue. The vast majority of Americans know that U.S. immigration laws should be sovereign, and not subject to disregard by millions, regardless of their need or aspirations. Immigration laws are designed to protect U.S. citizens by ensuring that permanent immigrants to this country do not have criminal backgrounds, do not have communicable diseases, and are sponsored by either employers or family members so they have support while in this country.

Moreover, illegal immigrants increase government spending on welfare, education, health systems and criminal justice. This is not racism; it is a well-researched fact.[150] Stated bluntly, our government is already in debt with entitlement obligations to citizens that it will never be able to provide. We simply cannot afford any non-citizens obtaining dependency status. A previous section in this book documented the destructive increase of dependency in America. Our economic survival requires we reduce this dependency, not enlarge it...regardless of race or culture.

If America is an evil, white, racist nation, why then are the vast majority of immigrants non-Caucasian? Why would they desire so desperately to get into the U.S.? Are they stupid? Self-delusional? No, of course they're not. They recognize that this is the land of opportunity and political freedom for every race. They cherish what native U.S. citizens take for granted and are so blithely voting away.

Neo-totalitarians are already tagging anyone who opposes the Obama government- expansion agenda, especially health care reform, as "racist". The leftist media is portraying Tea Party activists, who advocate only for reduced federal bureaucracy and spending, as being motivated by racism. Black conservatives (and there are many) are labeled as "Uncle Toms" or "BINOs" (Black In

Name Only). This tactic is, of course, straight out of the *Rules for Radicals* playbook. Please think carefully about this smear. These claims of racism assume that the federal government expansion is designed to benefit only specific races. Moreover, and even more insidious, this use of the "race card" presupposes that minority races are incapable of survival and improvement unless subsidized by more and more federal spending. This should be rejected as demeaning, untrue, counter-productive and arrogant.

Citizens of all races who act in good faith and desire to be informed on the issues should recognize the political desperation of such claims. If they do not, if they believe and legitimize them, then we are only further dividing ourselves to our ultimate despair and destruction.

In this regard, Conservatives have taken (and must continue to take) the high road to avoid even the slightest nuance of racial rhetoric. Conservatives must not appeal to what can be given, they have to appeal to what can be achieved. (Again, the U.S. military is the great example.) The American Dream pie will shrink for everyone, both producers and consumers, if it is confiscated and then "spread" to achieve "equality". The American Dream pie can only grow if it is fed by increasing numbers of producers and achievers of all races. The only beneficiaries from spreading the wealth are the elites that do the spreading, not the unfortunate political serfs that receive their largesse.

The best way to enlist minorities in the cause of patriotism is to speak the truth and leave the decision to each man and woman. Assume first, that they are industrious, rational, thinking individuals who can act in their own best interests, and are not automatons of the state responding only to handouts and racial stimuli.

Furthermore, Conservatives need to resist every attack by the Left, and their captive media accusing us of heartlessness, racism, division, or wanting to shred the social safety net. Do not respond if it only diverts, obfuscates and dilutes our focus on values. Do not try to "win" minorities by offering the same promises of dependency given by the Neo-totalitarian. You can never "out-entitle" them. They are the professional "tax and spenders". They will call your bluff and then raise the ante by creating another crisis or need that must be fixed. Speak only the truth. Neo-totalitarianism promises servitude. Patriotism and American values promise true freedom and prosperity.

The Republican Party at every level should engage the leaders of minority communities in discussions of specific issues of real and immediate impact. Offer to work side by side with these leaders to find real solutions to real problems that are destructive to minority communities. Problems such as high school drop-out rates, unwed pregnancy, drug abuse, crime and generational welfare dependency. Propose solutions built around self-sufficiency, self-reliance, and independence.

President Barack Obama himself is prima-facie evidence of the reality and impact of American values. Born in very humble circumstances, of mixed race before it was socially acceptable, abandoned by his father, partially raised by grandparents, moved not just from one location to another, but from one culture to another. He was a poverty statistic waiting to happen. He was primed to claim victimhood. He rejected that mantle, rejected dependency, and instead committed himself to education and self-development.

His success story is the embodiment of American values. His election as President is testimony to the fact that racism is dying in this country. President Obama could have been the ultimate role model for an entire generation by promulgating traditional American values of patriotism, self-reliance, meritorious achievement and thrift. It is simply ironic, and ultimately tragic for America, that his politics embrace Neo-totalitarianism, wealth redistribution, governmental dependency and class warfare.

Fully one third of American citizens today are non-Caucasian. The very concept of a "minority group" will, in a few short years, have very little meaning in our country. If we are to survive as a nation, the label that must transcend all others is *American*. We are all Americans. We all have a vested interest in a prosperous nation, a thriving economy and a secure future for our children.

Independents, the Center-Right and the Politically Uninformed

Often pundits declare that we are a "Center-right" country. Obama is said to have tailored his presidential campaign to appear centrist, and thus appeal to those in the Center Right. In large measure, the "Center-Right" voter is largely a myth. It is more accurately a semi-mathematical average of the views of all our citizens, amalgamated into a pithy description.

More specifically, there are millions of citizen-voters who simply defy categorization. They are true Independents[151]. Their positions transcend those of either end of the political spectrum. Their beliefs and preferences on specific issues are more eclectic. There are a great many Millennials and Gen-X voters in this category.

This is true particularly when addressing legislation dealing with issues of morality. Independents tend to be more socially progressive. For example, Independents may feel that abortion is morally wrong, and that they personally would not make that choice, but just as strongly feel that it is not their business or the government's business to prevent, encourage (or pay for) what must be a gut-wrenching personal decision for the person who has to make it.

Independents probably hold traditional views concerning marriage, and typically believe that marriage is between a man and woman, but also believe that this issue is not for the government to decide. Independents are much more concerned with the economic future of the country that their children will inherit than they are with other folk's morals .

Independents more than likely have religious beliefs, but do not place those beliefs at the forefront of their political priorities. However, and somewhat conversely, Independents resent and reject efforts by the Left to demean and de-legitimize our right to public religious expression.

Independents are typically proud of our strong military and that it can be used to protect and defend if needed. Police and humanitarian efforts, such as those in the Balkans, are generally applauded.

However, many Independents disapproved of the fact that the Bush Administration hurled our military against an Iraqi "enemy" without clear provocation, and "saved" a country that resents us, seems to be unappreciative of the democracy we sacrificed to give them, wants us to leave, and throws shoes at our President. Moreover, Independents are truly disgusted with the hypocrisy of those congresspersons who unanimously voted to invade Iraq and then, when the going got tough, sanctimoniously declared the war to be a "lost cause" and demanded withdrawal and abandonment. Independents are not quitters.

Independents are fiscally conservative and more likely to focus on fiscal prudence and common sense in domestic affairs. They are deeply concerned about the level of federal spending and debt. They worry about the opportunities and freedom their children will enjoy. Independent voters believe in paying their fair share of taxes, but resent supporting dependency. They believe in charity, but not by the government.

Independents disapprove of the current partisan divide and incivility in the national discourse. As a group, Independents desire political cooperation rather than conflict. Many voted for Barack Obama in 2008 seeking that cooperative spirit.

As simple as it sounds, the best way to win Independents is.... to speak the truth. Promise that our nation will step back from the brink of totalitarianism and return to American values and common sense. Promise a resurgence of freedom in America. Focus on the pressing economic, fiscal, entitlement and national defense problems we face. Demonstrate moral principles in decision-making, and recognize our Judeo-Christian heritage. Convince them that the wave of the future is not to join with the "progressives" but to join with the patriots. As the Neo-totalitarians are marginalized, perhaps the

Independents will view a merger with the majority of Americans who see themselves as Conservative as the most effective path toward cooperation and national unity.

Politically uninformed voters, on the other hand....are not stupid, they simply do not have the time or energy or motivation to read and understand issues. They don't do their homework. They depend on others to provide opinions when needed. They tend to agree and follow the political path of their friends and colleagues, and ultimately their socioeconomic or racial peers. They all too often react to media sound bites. Many simply do not care about politics, until it impacts them personally and directly. Many consider themselves as political "moderates" simply because they are ignorant of the issues that define any other political stance.

As conservatism flourishes and begins to sway the Independent voters, I believe the uninformed will follow along. They will hear the growing conservative voices of their family members and their peers at work, in school meetings, at church, in the tavern, on the softball team, in the neighborhood, in the union hall. Wherever folks get together, it will be difficult to avoid, whether they join the party or not. These new voices, however, will re-define the issues for the politically uninformed. While they may not have the time or desire to closely follow politics, everyone has family, friends and associates. For someone who does not have strong political inclinations, they will still pay attention to friends or trusted associates who do.

Part Five:
Real Hope

The Best Hope -- A New Republican Party

The post-Reagan Republican Party tried to be too many things, to too many people. All too often, political considerations drove policy, rather than values, principles and constituent needs. Deficit spending, expansion of Medicare entitlements, and immigration "reform" are all political quagmires that moved us in the wrong direction. Somewhere in the late 1990's, Republicans lost their copy of the *Contract with America*. Without it, sections of the Party became disenchanted and clamored for change, or outright separation.

Even though a separate "third party" may be attractive...practically speaking, it would simply divide Conservatives and empower Neo-totalitarians. We must never forget how Ross Perot divided Republican voters in 1992, and ushered in the 'magical' Clinton years.

For this reason, it is imperative that Republicans maintain a strong united front. To rally our forces, we must create a solid platform of patriotism and a return to core American values. This platform, composed of specific "position statements", freely and openly published, should form a rock solid foundation on which to govern. Republicans must not fall prey to any temptation to pander to every interest group or dilute fundamental principles in an effort to "widen the base" or "attract minorities". We must have confidence in our ability to attract voters, from any demographic, by governing with integrity. Republicans must adopt bold, clear-cut positions to define how the Party will lead the country back from the abyss, and into a new future. We must communicate this message to the public simply, continuously and boldly.

As a starting point, what could be bolder than for Republicans to adopt the New Hampshire state motto: "Live Free or Die" as a symbol of our resolve? That might raise temperatures faster than a "global warming" report on CNN, and far more interesting to watch. (General John Stark, by the way, was one of Washington's generals during the Revolutionary War. He wrote the famous words "Live Free or Die" in a letter to his military comrades in 1809. It became the official New Hampshire state motto in 1945).

From our Revolutionary beginnings, to the present day, our representative form of government was designed for constituents to demand action from their office holders, those who represented *them*. It has always been the intent that constituent needs should take precedence over isolation, self-interest or blind obedience to party dogma. So what do constituents need with more dogma?

What you are about to read, is what a Republican platform could be -- a new "Promise for America". This clearly stated "Promise" would allow not only constituents, but all voters across the country, to examine and evaluate policy differences between the Democrat Party and the patriotic "Party of the Republic". Armed with this knowledge, Americans will be able to wisely choose a promising future for our country; without it, the choices may not be as wise.

There is one caveat; when you promise something, you must do it. Any school-kid knows this; some of our unscrupulous leaders do not. Therefore, honest, principled and determined leadership will be crucial, if Republicans are to live the "Promise" and become the "Party that Saved America". However, if we were to be given the privilege of leading both Congress and the Presidency, and then *fail* to govern according to those promises, we will never survive...we will deserve to wither and die.

Accordingly, Republicans must stand united. If we fail to turn the totalitarian tide, it is likely that American Conservatives will lose all patience. True Conservatives will abandon us and form a third party, or run as Independents, and divert so many votes from Republican candidates, that neither will win.

Republicans must find a leader for every post, including the Presidency, who is a warrior/patriot. One who is strong enough to stand on core principles, courageous enough to withstand the Leftist media onslaught, young enough at heart to attract Millennials, and able to articulate issues adroitly, without being a teleprompter parrot. One who can unite traditional Republicans, Tea Partiers, solid Conservatives, Independents and Libertarians, under the *Promise for America* banner. I have faith that those warrior/patriots are out there.

The Promise for America

The Republican Party will offer a clear and definitive choice for the American people. Republicans will provide leadership that will be crucial in guiding our country back to prosperity, and away from the governmental engorgement policies of President Obama and Congressional Democrats. We will offer common sense solutions based on core American principles and values in the following crucial areas. These promises are not intended to address every problem, issue or concern in America. Instead, they are intended to focus on those that are the most immediate and important to our national future. Let us fix these.....then we'll get to others.

1. Never Apologize For American Greatness

Republicans believe that we are blessed to live in the most amazing nation on earth.

Our current President, to the delight of his Neo-totalitarian supporters and our international detractors, has humiliated our county and apologized for our exceptionalism. All in the name of a doctrine of "engagement", which has proven to be a failure. President Obama has offered contrite apologies to Muslims, to Europeans and to our neighbors in the Americas. He has accused the United States of making mistakes, of arrogance, of being dismissive, of being disengaged, of even dictating our terms.

This must stop! The Republican Party will not apologize for the greatness of our nation. There is no need. There is not now, nor has there ever been a country like the United States. We have, through sacrifices of lives and treasure, done more to bring freedom and prosperity to the world than any other country in history. We take on the thankless task of leadership in a dangerous world. We have always shouldered the hardest burdens. Accomplishing these things relies on strength of character, integrity, resolve, faith and determination -- not international popularity.

2. Face Our Economic Challenge

Republicans steadfastly believe in the inherent strength of our American free-market economy. We believe that real wealth and prosperity is earned, not "redistributed". Republicans believe that our current economic challenges are not due to a failure of free-market capitalism nor were they caused by deregulation of government control. Federal stimulus spending and programs have offered nothing more than a temporary "Band-Aid" and have mired us in a political economy which destroys opportunity and incentives for all. In addition, they have failed to restore vibrant activity in our economy, or allowed our citizens to have any greater confidence in the economic future of our country.

Republicans will focus on free-market policies to create real jobs and reduce unemployment. Returning people to work is a crucial prerequisite to reversing our housing crisis. This does not mean laisser-faire hands-off regulation. Indeed, we believe in safeguards -- but not handcuffs.

We strongly contend that the current era of uncertainty about what the federal government will do next (in terms of taxes and regulation) is preventing businesses large and small from creating new jobs to replace those lost during the recession. With national unemployment near 10% (and the real total unemployment rate near 17%), we simply cannot afford a "jobless" recovery -- if indeed we are in the process of a real recovery at all. Republicans will end this era of uncertainty and fear by stopping planned tax increases, repealing health care mandates and draconian financial regulation, and preventing job-killing climate regulations. Government spending reductions, balanced budgets, debt reduction, and tax reform are all crucial elements to restoring confidence and vitality in our economy.

3. Stop The Spending Madness -- Starve the Beast

Reform the Tax System

The current U.S. tax system penalizes the qualities that make America great: thrift, saving, investing and risk taking. The tax code is also ridiculously complex. Today, uncertainty and globalization compound this threat to our economy.

If the tax relief enacted in 2001 and 2003 is allowed to expire, come January 1, 2011, all income tax rates will increase dramatically across the board; capital gains and dividends taxes will rise; the child tax credit will be cut by 50%; the marriage tax penalty will resume; and the death tax will be back in full force. Add all this up, and American taxpayers will get hit with a $300 billion tax increase in that and every year thereafter – the largest tax increase in the history of the world! As of this writing, Congress has not been able to agree on if and how taxes will increase.

On top of this, is the escalating problem of the Alternative Minimum Tax (AMT), which was never indexed to account for inflation and is affecting growing numbers, millions, of middle-income American families. Recently, the Democratic Chairman of the House Ways and Means Committee unveiled a plan that trades one bad tax for another – repealing the AMT but replacing this illegitimate tax with other taxes – including a surtax that falls squarely on America's small businesses. Suffice it to say, the plan's $3.5 trillion in tax hikes over ten years wouldn't help us compete in a global economy with emerging powers such as China and India.

Our current system of taxation and revenue collection by Washington is the product of a century of tinkering by tax lawyers, lobbyists, special interests, Congress, the IRS and corporations looking to erect barriers to their competitors. These policies are destructive and we couldn't disagree with them more.

We believe the tax code should be scrapped and replaced with a system that is flatter, fairer, and simpler. Our tax system should reward success, not punish it. It should encourage saving, investing and risk-taking, instead of taxing it. Businesses should make decisions based on what is best for business and their customers, not what is best for their tax return. Allowing the federal government to pick winners and losers through the tax code is reckless and counter-productive.

At a time when we are facing unprecedented global economic challenges, our tax system should not be pushing jobs and capital overseas; it should make America the best place in the world to invest capital, grow jobs and start businesses. We believe our tax system should, at most, tax income once, at its source, and never again -- no tax on capital gains, no tax on dividends, no tax on death. Better yet, how about a tax system that rewards all those things we say we want, like diligence, ingenuity, perseverance, success, entrepreneurship? How about not taxing income at all? This form of taxation inherently decreases productivity and places a drag on economic expansion.

Taxes on American businesses are among the highest in the world. The top corporate tax rate in the United States is 40 percent. In Ireland it is 12.5 percent, in Hungary it is 16 percent. Even Germany's tax rate is lower than ours at 38.4 percent. In fact, of the 30 major countries in the world, only Japan has a higher rate than the United States at 40.7 percent.

Our tax system should be border adjustable so our exports can compete and our imports are treated equally. Businesses should have immediate expensing and no more convoluted and irrational depreciation schedules.

There is no other single factor that determines the growth and success of a nation's economy more than its tax code. Ours is obsolete and downright destructive. America can and should lead the world in the 21st century to a dynamic, prosperous and free global economy. And by leading the way, we will help those who have not seen hope, growth and prosperity see the future and come to realize personally what is known as the "American dream."

Restore Fiscal Discipline

The federal budget must not grow faster than American families' ability to pay for it. The amount government spends annually per household has risen to more than $23,000 per household. The current share of the national debt for every American is over $42,000. Even more ominously, the present value of unfunded obligations for the federal government is equal to $440,000 per household. It is not plausible to tax our way to reducing this level, instead we must restrain spending. No more unwanted or unneeded new programs, no more spending increases without spending offsets, and no more earmarks.

Balance the Budget

A crucial step in our economic policy must include balancing the federal budget. This must be done through spending reductions. Ultimately, Republicans favor a Constitutional Amendment to force balanced federal budgets, and so do I. Never again can we provide politicians the means to print money or create massive debt.

Change the Budgeting Process

The federal budgeting process makes it far too easy for the federal budget to encroach upon the family budget. We are committed to changing the federal budget process to reverse these priorities. The current budget process should be converted to a simple and legally binding document while also placing ceilings on discretionary and automatic spending. We must also place a premium on reducing spending without cutting needed services, by combating waste, fraud, and abuse through sunset

requirements, transparency and accountability, and a legislative line item veto.
Leverage Privatization

Republicans believe we should decrease the federal workforce and increase the use of private contractors to reduce public spending. Federal bureaucrats become like tenured faculty -- self-sustaining and impossible to fire. Increasing the use of private business will forge real savings through competition and the inherent efficiency of U.S. enterprise. Unit cost contracts, in particular, offer huge opportunities for savings, if managed properly. Private contractors are currently used successfully in critical functions such as state prison management and in such routine tasks as municipal trash collection. The opportunities for financial savings are substantial.

Republicans believe that we need to consider innovative uses of contractors to address some of our current intractable problems. For example, private audit companies could be used to attack the waste and fraud that are rampant in Medicare and Medicaid, and could be paid from a small percentage of savings, thus costing taxpayers nothing and potentially saving billions. Or consider using private companies to manage a national guest worker program to match the workforce needs of American industry with legal temporary immigrants. The U.S. companies would gladly pay the fees associated with such a program.

4. Fundamental Entitlement Reform

No three programs define the domestic mission of the federal government of the 20th century more than Social Security, Medicare, and Medicaid. These programs were created during difficult times and were designed to bring retirement and health security to low income and old age Americans; and for a while, they worked well for recipients. Today, nearly 50 million Americans rely on Social Security and Medicare and 38 million receive their health care through Medicaid.

Unfortunately, this system is going bankrupt. What's more, these three programs alone will consume 100% of the federal budget by the year 2040. Today they consume 60%. Because these programs operate on a pay-as-you-go basis, where current workers pay taxes to fund current beneficiaries, the ratio of worker to retiree will require the tax burden of the next generation of American workers to double simply to keep the status quo afloat.

Clearly, this is not a viable system. America's retirement population is increasing by 100% while the working and taxpaying population is increasing by only 17%. According to the General Accountability Office, rather than taxing 18% of the U.S. Gross Domestic Product to finance the federal government (as it does today), these three programs will require a federal tax burden of 40% of GDP by 2040, simply to pay for today's commitments.

Americans cannot succeed and compete with such a crushing tax burden. America will lose its greatness. The legacy of leaving the next generation with a higher standard of living will be lost. This must not happen.

We can do better.

We believe in the mission of retirement and health security. We think there are better solutions that give Americans the comfort of knowing their health care and retirement is secure by giving people ownership and control over such critical components of their lives. While millions of Americans have organized their lives around Medicare and Social Security, the guarantee of such benefits is only what Congress deems them to be in any given year. That's neither fair or good enough, especially with the future wave of generational friction that is mounting.

Washington has proven itself incapable of managing Americans' hard earned Social Security dollars. For example, under the current budget resolution, the federal government would spend at least a portion of the Social Security surplus for other federal spending every single year. This is robbing from Peter to pay Paul. With Social Security facing near-term financial difficulties, this is unacceptable. It should be against the law to spend Social Security money collected from Americans on anything other than Social Security.

We support a plan to transform this 20th century entitlement system into a 21st century ownership system where citizens have real property rights to their health and retirement benefits. People should be able to build a nest egg that provides them with better benefits that are much more secure than a politician's promise. The mission of health and retirement security can be realized by building a new system where people can own and increase their savings throughout their working years so they can rely on the retirement benefits that they are not only entitled to, but that they own.

Our goal is to transform this pay-as-you-go system into a fully funded system that harnesses the power of individual incentives, compound interest, patient-centered health care and converts this current multi-trillion dollar liability into a national asset where Americans continue to enjoy ever higher standards of living.

Welfare Reform

We must stop continuation of welfare dependence from one generation to the next. As shown in a previous section of this work, the level of dependence on government by individuals has grown to alarming and destructive proportions. Previous efforts at welfare reform had remarkable success. From 1996 to 2008, welfare caseloads declined by 62%. Over one million children were lifted out of poverty by welfare to work programs. However, too many welfare programs still depend on means-tested eligibility, without a plan to break dependence. Moreover, the American Recovery and Reinvestment Act of 2009 essentially overturned formerly successful welfare reform, reverting to a funding scheme that rewards swelling the welfare rolls.

Republicans support simplification and streamlining of the number of programs and the level of bureaucracy involved in providing temporary support to Americans. We support positive, clearly defined limits on the duration of welfare payments, and the requirement that recipients work. We reject current programs that encourage non-work, encourage unwed motherhood, and penalize marriage.

5. Stop Making Promises We Can't Keep

Public Confidence in the Integrity of Elected Officials Is Essential To Our Nation

Americans deserve to have elected officials who represent them, including Members of Congress, abide by the highest possible standards of professional conduct and personal ethics. No Member of Congress should engage in any activity in which there is or could be a conflict of interest between his or her official duties or activities on behalf of his constituents and any personal interest of that Member. This duty to avoid conflicts of interest is critical to public confidence in the integrity of our nation's government. To effectuate this duty, Members must aggressively avoid any conflict of interest and must actively support transparency of action.

Recognizing this critical duty, House Republicans in 1994 pledged to "re-establish the bonds of trust between the United States Congress and the American people." Regrettably, we failed to achieve and maintain this goal. Now Congress must reinvigorate its efforts to reestablish those bonds of trust and hold every Member to a zero tolerance standard in which no self-dealing or impropriety whatsoever will be tolerated.

Eliminate Earmarks

One of the main culprits of self-dealing is the practice of "earmarking." The 1981 transportation bill contained only 10 earmarks. President Reagan vetoed a transportation bill in 1987 that contained 121 earmarks, saying, *'I haven't seen this much lard since I handed out blue ribbons at the Iowa State Fair.'* In 2005, Congress passed a transportation bill that included an astonishing 6,371 earmarks at a cost of $27.3 billion.

The year before Republicans took the majorities in the U.S. House and U.S. Senate, there were 1,400 earmarks. Last year, there were more than 14,000. Republicans believe that until public confidence is restored, we must end all earmarks. To lead by example, Republican Congressional members have committed to requesting no new earmarks in the current 111th Congress. Absolute transparency and accountability in reforming this broken system is imperative.

6. Health Care Reform

Patient Choices

America deserves a health care system which ensures that every American receives patient-centered health care services, while preserving the ability of individuals and their families to make their own decisions about their health care, including the doctors they use and the facilities and drugs they have available, and does so at an affordable cost. No American should go without necessary health care services.

The federal government should enact policies which ensure all Americans receive the care they need.

The current system takes patients out of the decision-making process and diminishes their incentive to take responsibility for their treatment decisions, wellness and preventive care. It must be reformed. This system punishes individuals who do not receive health care through their employer by requiring them to pay for health care with after-tax dollars. It creates a discriminatory tax advantage for those who receive employer-funded health care by allowing employers to pay for that care with pre-tax dollars. This inequity cannot be allowed to continue.

While employers have an interest in the well-being of their employees, the primary responsibility and decision-making authority should rest with patients, in consultation with their families and doctors. Employers should be encouraged to continue helping their employees, but all Americans should be treated equally regardless of whether they get their health care through their employer or not.

Health Coverage for All

To ensure that all Americans have health coverage, there is a relatively simple and easy method that would allow every American to receive a tax deduction or credit for their family or individual health insurance coverage. For those Americans who need further assistance, a tax credit may be advanceable and/or refundable so that all may be able to gain coverage that they believe most appropriate for themselves, not that which the government dictates to you.

The beauty of this is that it would provide for a system that makes it financially feasible and attractive for everyone to purchase their health coverage, and financially foolish for anyone not to do so. This system will empower both patients and doctors while ensuring that all Americans receive appropriate health care.

End Third-party control

The current system places too many decisions in the hands of third-party payers, e.g., employers and insurance providers. Similarly, America should not adopt a system of government-run, 'single-payer' (socialized medicine) like Canada and Britain, as advocated by many, empowering government and government bureaucrats to make health care decisions, rationing care and under-compensating providers. Every Democrat candidate for President in the last cycle promoted one form or another of socialized medicine. Such a system will further damage patient choices, empower bureaucrats and ration care to control costs. We believe that is exactly the wrong policy for America. We can do better. And, we must.

7. Education

Raise the standard of elementary and secondary education by reinstating parental involvement, restoring local control, expanding flexibility and choices, and eliminating the bureaucratic barriers to ensure that every child receives a quality education.

The single greatest influence on educational success is the involvement of parents in their children's education.

When Congress passed the 2001 No Child Left Behind Act (NCLB), they stripped the ability of schools to innovatively and creatively meet individual student needs. For the first time the federal government was given permission to dictate school curriculum by mandating testing, performance and creating sanctions for schools that failed to meet federal standards.

The unintended consequences of NCLB have led to increased paperwork, teachers feeling pressure to teach to the tests, elimination of subjects not part of the core curriculum and schools trying to restrict certain students from enrolling in their school for fear they may negatively impact their ability to meet state standards.

Through NCLB, Washington has severed the bond between parents, local schools and communities making effective education of our children nearly impossible.

We stand for providing students the opportunity to receive an excellent education that permits innovation and freedom from excessive burdens and regulations. We support the return of education to state and local government and we support parental choice. Parents, not bureaucrats, are the most qualified to determine where their child should attend school.

We stand for education tax credits and educational opportunity scholarships that will empower parents. Tax credits give parents and communities the opportunity to contribute directly toward educational needs rather than having their money funneled through Washington and spent on priorities set by government bureaucrats. Opportunity scholarships give parents the tools to choose the school that will best teach and enrich their children.

We understand that the best approach to meeting local educational needs is to eliminate red tape and the ineffective federal government bureaucracy. Congress needs to provide parents, teachers, school principals and communities with the freedom to chart a new course for local schools designed to best meet local students' needs.

We need to ask ourselves a fundamental question: Who will decide the future of our children's education? Faceless bureaucrats in Washington? Or parents and local school administrators who know our children's names and needs? The answer is clear.

8. Immigration

The United States is a land of opportunity, founded on the radical notion of *E Pluribus Unum*: "From many, comes

One." As such, this nation has always welcomed immigrants, regardless of national origin.

After Congress passed immigration reform in 1986, the federal government did not live up to its promises of enforcement and border security. As a result, the United States is facing its current illegal immigration crisis.

It is the responsibility of the federal government to control our borders and ports of entry and, in doing so, regain the trust of the American people. Then, and only then, should Congress proceed with more comprehensive immigration reform. Amnesty, the granting of citizenship to anyone here illegally, is unacceptable.

Getting a handle on today's crisis must begin with enforcing the rule of law and ensuring border security. It means creating a force multiplier by dedicating more resources to state and local law enforcement so that they can assist federal efforts.

Illegal aliens are drawn to the United States in the hope of economic prosperity, but our workforce must not be stocked through unlawful workers. Ultimately this serves to undermine legal American workers. Businesses must have a reliable and immediate means to verify a worker's eligibility. Immigration control is the government's job, not the employer's.

Businesses which refuse to stop hiring cheap, illegal labor must face stiff financial penalties. However, once border security is confirmed, the entire debate becomes much more productive and positive. The federal government must then reform its current worker visa programs in order to be more consumer and employer-friendly and meet the needs of today's dynamic economy.

It is time to end the comfort zone that has been created for illegal aliens to remain in the United States through a multitude of benefits and incentives. Just being in this country should not entitle one to free health care, a line of credit or tax benefits – all things that Americans work and pay for every day.

The success of the United States as a melting pot is based on immigrants assimilating into a common identity and obeying the law. To ensure that newcomers are not separated from the mainstream, English must be adopted as the official language and bilingual education and ballots phased out.

9. Energy

More and more Americans are focused on the issue of climate change and trying to determine whether it is real, and if so, whether human activity is the cause. Science generally shows that the earth is warming slightly. The unsettled question, and the cause of the most passionate debate, is whether so-called greenhouse gases, including CO_2, are the cause.

The answer to this problem is to begin immediately to improve our energy efficiency; take reasonable steps to reduce greenhouse gases and carbon dioxide emissions; explore alternative fuels; reduce our reliance on fossil fuels and foreign sources of energy and continue appropriate research. We should not undertake measures which will destroy American jobs. Unnecessary compliance costs are certain to be passed on to consumers while the payoffs they will provide are unclear and unproven, especially as we are working toward alternative forms of energy and lessening our dependence on foreign oil.

We stand for American energy security – because there is no silver bullet, America cannot afford to shut off any avenue that might lead us toward that goal.

More must be done to encourage and educate the American people to conserve and use our energy resources as efficiently and effectively as possible. Our American Energy Innovation Act of 2009 provided for an 'All of the Above' energy plan, including incentives for responsible conservation. Energy conservation is a key to achieving energy independence. These types of incentives can be excellent building blocks toward that end.

We must also increase domestic production. In the short term we cannot ignore domestic supplies that are available to us and continue to pour money into hostile regimes that don't support America's goals and interests. Increased domestic production can help buy time for innovation in new technologies and decrease our foreign oil dependence. The recent disaster in the Gulf of Mexico demonstrates the clear need for aggressive and responsible oversight. However, if it is used to put in place public policy that markedly diminishes our ability to appropriately utilize our vast resources, we will further jeopardize not just our energy security, but our national security as well.

We should encourage innovation by providing incentives for advancement in hydrogen and fuel cell technology as well as clean nuclear power. Providing incentives for business to develop and create alternative fuel technologies is part of the solution.

No nuclear power plant has been built in the U.S. in over 25 years. We must begin immediately to build clean, third-generation nuclear power generating stations. We must also reduce cumbersome regulations that have led to boutique fuels which unnecessarily tighten supplies and create price spikes. This is a major factor in why gas prices increase dramatically during the summer driving months. Responsibly streamlining regulations is also the first step in allowing industry to build new refineries.

We must improve our domestic infrastructure, build more refineries and pipelines, and increase our capacity to get more product to market. Science will also provide solutions that are yet unknown.

Finally, there are enormous benefits to energy security. It will ensure that our economy remains strong, help stabilize energy prices, end our subsidizing of regimes whose interests conflict with America's and provide us with greater flexibility in foreign policy.

10. National Security

Americans have long embraced the challenge of securing our nation against our enemies, and we remain dedicated to delivering a safe and secure America to future generations. The threat we face today is unlike any in our history and cannot be overstated. Failure is not an option. Radical Jihadists are devoted to eradicating free societies and replacing them with an archaic and dangerous theocratic rule under strict Sha'ria law.

Because America's love for freedom and innate idealism go counter to this strict, extremist ideology, we are the primary target for Radical Jihadists' violent actions. We understand that an adaptive military and intelligence community is necessary to aggressively engage these extremists abroad in order to succeed in preserving our American way of life at home. We understand that this is a global "war" and that current areas of conflict are central fronts.

For 50 years, during the Cold War, we had a defined strategy against a nuclear Soviet Union, and we were ultimately triumphant. Filling the vacuum of evil created by the defeat of Soviet totalitarianism are rogue radical Islamists intent on imposing their Sha'ria law in which religious power is inseparable from political, military and state power.

Recognizing that they cannot match America's military power through traditional military means, this enemy has posed an asymmetrical attack characterized by indiscriminate, ruthless, usually unpredictable acts of destruction. These people who have vowed to spread this archaic Muslim theocracy are murderers and thugs who wear no uniform and will stop at nothing to create their desired reality.

On September 11, 2001 we were given a glimpse of the chaos and death they hope to deliver onto Americans unwilling to submit to their ideology. But these cold-blooded terrorists do not rely solely on large-scale attacks. They are willing to detonate bombs strapped to the undercarriage of cars and the chests of their children in order to deliver their message and defeat our will.

We refuse to see the American people live under the fear that when our children go to the mall they may encounter a suicide bomber. The Sha'ria law that these jihadists are violently spreading promotes a society where women are accorded no rights and must conceal themselves, alleged criminals are not afforded the presumption of innocence but are beheaded, and where wars are ultimately conducted to force conversion to Islam.

Al-Qaeda and terrorist-sponsoring, rogue regimes such as Iran and Syria will continue to try to destroy our way of life with individual acts of terrorism, all while seeking nuclear and biological weapons that can kill Americans *en masse*. We are waging the first battles in a war against American freedom and idealism that may last for decades. America must remain militarily strong and diplomatically engaged to once again prevail.

We also understand that covert action is imperative in a world with so many dangers. An unrealistic view by any elected official of the very real threat before us is reckless and irresponsible. Resolve of duty and action is imperative and will be more than welcomed by a citizenry skeptical of either by many currently in office.

A Final Word

Let not your heart be troubled....
Book of John, Chapter 14, Verse 1.

If you are a Conservative patriot reading this book, you may feel a sense of hopelessness. The damage to our beloved country may seem irreversible, the ability of individuals to affect meaningful and lasting change may seem remote. There is no doubt that our task will be difficult and the road back from totalitarianism will be long.

But do not forget, we are Americans. Our greatest strength is courage in the face of daunting odds. Throughout our history, individual Americans and groups of Americans have overcome "insurmountable" obstacles simply because we refused to fail. We beat down our fear, we inspire those around us, we work tirelessly, we fight tenaciously, we overcome suffering. We ignore the naysayers and defeatists, and just persevere.

Thomas Paine encouraged our revolutionary war patriots with these words: *The harder the conflict, the more glorious the triumph. What we obtain too cheap, we esteem too lightly; it is dearness only that gives everything its value. I love the man that can smile in trouble, that can gather strength from distress and grow.*

Need more inspiration?

Most of today's citizens are unfamiliar with the reality of our Revolutionary War. Our victory and subsequent independence from Britain was literally a miracle -- there can be no other description. A ragtag, underfed, under-equipped band of regulars and militia challenged the most powerful, well-armed and well-trained Army and Navy on earth. In late fall of 1776, George Washington's army suffered defeat after humiliating defeat. They were running to avoid destruction and capture. Desertions were rampant. Loyalists were ridiculing any Continentals who continued to fight, and were ingratiating themselves to the soon-to-be-victorious British. No one expected the rebels to survive the coming winter. Defeat of the Continental army meant that our founding fathers, the signers of the Declaration and the officers leading the fight, would be hanged as traitors to the Crown.

As freezing weather closed in, our fighting men were in pitiful shape. Forty percent had no boots or shoes in the ice and snow. This is not a fairytale. Imagine the desperation these men felt. George Washington knew he had one last chance -- one desperate gamble before his "army" simply evaporated and the revolution died.

This warrior/leader is called the Father of Our Country for a reason. Making the bold decision, and taking full responsibility, Washington, the commanding General, personally led his men on a dangerous overnight crossing of the Delaware River, and then a sleet-plagued, miles-long trek to attempt a Christmas Day surprise attack on the tough Hessian mercenaries that occupied Trenton, N.J. His soldiers thought the attack was suicidal, but such was Washington's leadership and integrity that they followed him anyway. These men not only defeated the Hessians, they achieved a complete rout, capturing much needed supplies, and sustaining the revolution. Imagine what our future and the future of the world would be if such an individual had not been there at that time and place.

Need more?

The Civil War ripped our country to pieces. In the crucial battlegrounds of the East, the Confederate Army of Northern Virginia, under Robert E. Lee's audacious tactics, achieved victory upon victory through the first two years of war. Losses on both sides were high, but the Union's losses were staggering. The citizens of the U.S. were growing weary of the sacrifice. Lincoln, determined at all costs to re-unite our country, desperately needed to win a battle simply to avoid a political backlash and loss of national will.

In July 1863, the Union and Confederate armies met at Gettysburg, Pennsylvania. Lee was gambling that a successful invasion of the North would hasten the Union's political collapse. He knew the Union commanding general he faced (George Meade) was not a warrior. On the second day of the battle, Lee truly unleashed his forces against a superior force of Federals. His tactic was to turn the Union's flank at the end of their line, attack their rear and drive them from the field. The end of their line of deployment was a small hill named Little Round Top.

Securing this hill was an unassuming college professor from Maine named Joshua Lawrence Chamberlain. He had no military background, but had been placed in command of a regiment of militia because he was educated. The 20th Maine was mostly untested and was placed on the extreme flank because Meade was convinced of an attack at the center. On that fateful second day of the crucial battle to determine the life or death of our United States, Chamberlain was tested. Assaulted multiple times by battle-hardened Alabama veterans, the Mainers were decimated and on the verge of collapse. The flank, the battle, the war, and the country hung in the balance. At the peak of the final attack, Chamberlain, knowing full well the consequences of failure, ordered and personally led a bayonet charge directly into the guns of the Alabamans. The Southerners, shocked and overwhelmed, fled. The battle raged on, but the flank was secured. Imagine a different future for our country were it not for one heroic individual.

More?

One of the saddest chapters in our history is the treatment of our Black citizens following their freedom from slavery after the Civil War. For decades, Blacks were not treated as equal citizens of America. There was harsh discrimination in education, employment and the marketplace. Many lived in poverty. The prospect of changing these conditions seemed almost impossible. The struggle for Black equality faced daunting legal and cultural barriers. Into this battle stepped a warrior/leader with a different tactic. In the 1950's, Martin Luther King, Jr. adopted Gandhi's philosophy of non-violent, civil disobedience to highlight and protest the wrongs many people endured. His eloquence, his coolness in the face of violent opposition, his bold courage in the face of danger inspired all he touched.   His tragic, heroic death galvanized his movement. What would we be as a nation without this one individual?

Last one....

Our country was in its deepest malaise since the Great Depression. We were dispirited and depressed. We had been humiliated by military defeat and betrayed by political corruption. Our economy was in shambles with low growth, high unemployment, rampant inflation, and record-level interest rates. No expert seemed to know how to attack it all. We were locked in a seemingly never-ending Cold War with an implacable enemy, whose communist system was conquering countries while we wrung our hands. We were not respected internationally. An oil cartel felt empowered to wreak economic havoc upon us. A small Middle Eastern country had held U.S citizens hostage for a year and we seemed powerless to rescue them. We had been told by our President that we had to begin to sacrifice our way of life.

One man had a vision of what America could be. He was ridiculed as too old. His patriotism was labeled as too old fashioned, his anti-Communist beliefs were called too confrontational. He was laughed at because he had been a second tier movie star and once co-starred with a chimp. But Ronald Reagan felt that his destiny was to lead America out of its dark decades. He defeated an incumbent president and began a quest to restore our economy, defeat our enemy and reinvigorate our national pride.

An assassin tried to kill him, and came closer than the nation knew, and he cracked jokes. Early in his first term, his economic policies came under immense pressure because the country entered a recession shortly after he took office, and unemployment soared. Displaying the bold courage that marked his Presidency, he withstood the pressure, persevered with his policies, and when he left office in 1989, inflation was minimal, interest rates had returned to normalcy, unemployment was low and our economy was in a growth phase that would last for more than a decade.

He launched a multi-faceted offensive against the 'evil empire'. Despite criticism, he rebuilt and restored our military strength from its post-Viet Nam low. He challenged the Soviets to match our military technological prowess, which he knew they could not accomplish. He met them face to face and forged a favorable arms reduction treaty. And he encouraged his Soviet counterpart to reform and restructure internally. He steadfastly believed that the march of freedom and economic prosperity would prevail over totalitarianism. One year after he left office, the U.S.S.R. collapsed.

Was he perfect? No. Did he make mistakes? Of course. But the United States would be a far worse country in a far more dangerous world if it had not been for the patriotic vision of one man, who came to us at the right time.

৪০০৪

These and countless other American heroes, call to us from history. We *can* save our country. We *can* begin the hard fight to transform the United States back into the Constitutional Republic that will ensure a strong and prosperous America for our children's future.

The time is now.

The crisis we are facing today....requires our best effort, and our willingness to believe in ourselves and to believe in our capacity to perform great deeds; to believe that together, with God's help, we can and will resolve the problems which now confront us. And, after all, why shouldn't we believe that? We are Americans.
---President Ronald Reagan

Appendix I

Not Yours to Give
by Colonel David Crockett;
Compiled by Edward S. Ellis
(Philadelphia: Porter & Coates, 1884)[152]

One day in the House of Representatives, a bill was taken up appropriating money for the benefit of a widow of a distinguished naval officer. Several beautiful speeches had been made in its support. The Speaker was just about to put the question when Crockett arose:

"Mr. Speaker, I have as much respect for the memory of the deceased, and as much sympathy for the sufferings of the living, if suffering there be, as any man in this House, but we must not permit our respect for the dead or our sympathy for a part of the living to lead us into an act of injustice to the balance of the living. I will not go into an argument to prove that Congress has no power to appropriate this money as an act of charity. Every member upon this floor knows it. We have the right, as individuals, to give away as much of our own money as we please in charity; but as members of Congress we have no right so to appropriate a dollar of the public money. Some eloquent appeals have been made to us upon the ground that it is a debt due the deceased. Mr. Speaker, the deceased lived long after the close of the war; he was in office to the day of his death, and I have never heard that the government was in arrears to him.

"Every man in this House knows it is not a debt. We cannot, without the grossest corruption, appropriate this money as the payment of a debt. We have not the semblance of authority to appropriate it as a charity. Mr. Speaker, I have said we have the right to give as much money of our own as we please. I am the poorest man on this floor. I cannot vote for this bill, but I will give one week's pay to the object, and if every member of Congress will do the same, it will amount to more than the bill asks."

He took his seat. Nobody replied. The bill was put upon its passage, and, instead of passing unanimously, as was generally supposed, and as, no doubt, it would, but for that speech, it received but few votes, and, of course, was lost.

Later, when asked by a friend why he had opposed the appropriation, Crockett gave this explanation:

"Several years ago I was one evening standing on the steps of the Capitol with some other members of Congress, when our attention was attracted by a great light over in Georgetown . It was evidently a large fire. We jumped into a hack and drove over as fast as we could. In spite of all that could be done, many houses were burned and many families made homeless, and, besides, some of them had lost all but the clothes they had on. The weather was very cold, and when I saw so many women and children suffering, I felt that something ought to be done for them. The next morning a bill was introduced appropriating $20,000 for their relief. We put aside all other business and rushed it through as soon as it could be done.

"The next summer, when it began to be time to think about the election, I concluded I would take a scout around among the boys of my district. I had no opposition there, but, as the election was some time off, I did not know what might turn up. When riding one day in a part of my district in which I was more of a stranger than any other, I saw a man in a field plowing and coming toward the road. I gauged my gait so that we should meet as he came to the fence. As he came up, I spoke to the man. He replied politely, but, as I thought, rather coldly.

"I began: 'Well, friend, I am one of those unfortunate beings called candidates, and-'

"'Yes, I know you; you are Colonel Crockett, I have seen you once before, and voted for you the last time you were elected. I suppose you are out electioneering now, but you had better not waste your time or mine. I shall not vote for you again.'

"This was a sockdolager . . . I begged him to tell me what was the matter.

"'Well, Colonel, it is hardly worth-while to waste time or words upon it. I do not see how it can be mended, but you gave a vote last winter which shows that either you have not capacity to understand the Constitution, or that you are wanting in the honesty and firmness to be guided by it. In either case you are not the man to represent me. But I beg your pardon for expressing it in that way. I did not intend to avail myself of the privilege of the constituent to speak plainly to a candidate for the purpose of insulting or wounding you. I intend by it only to say that your understanding of the Constitution is very different from mine; and I will say to you what, but for my rudeness, I should not have said, that I believe you to be honest. . . . But an understanding of the Constitution different from mine I cannot overlook, because the Constitution, to be worth anything, must be held sacred, and rigidly observed in all its provisions. The man who wields power and misinterprets it is the more dangerous the more honest he is.'

184 | Saving The American Miracle

"'I admit the truth of all you say, but there must be some mistake about it, for I do not remember that I gave any vote last winter upon any constitutional question.'

"'No, Colonel, there's no mistake. Though I live here in the backwoods and seldom go from home, I take the papers from Washington and read very carefully all the proceedings of Congress. My papers say that last winter you voted for a bill to appropriate $20,000 to some sufferers by a fire in Georgetown. Is that true?'

"'Well, my friend; I may as well own up. You have got me there. But certainly nobody will complain that a great and rich country like ours should give the insignificant sum of $20,000 to relieve its suffering women and children, particularly with a full and overflowing Treasury, and I am sure, if you had been there, you would have done just as I did.'

"'It is not the amount, Colonel, that I complain of; it is the principle. In the first place, the government ought to have in the Treasury no more than enough for its legitimate purposes. But that has nothing to do with the question. The power of collecting and disbursing money at pleasure is the most dangerous power that can be intrusted to man, particularly under our system of collecting revenue by a tariff, which reaches every man in the country, no matter how poor he may be, and the poorer he is the more he pays in proportion to his means. What is worse, it presses upon him without his knowledge where the weight centers, for there is not a man in the United States who can ever guess how much he pays to the government. So you see, that while you are contributing to relieve one, you are drawing it from thousands who are even worse off than he. If you had the right to give anything, the amount was simply a matter of discretion with you, and you had as much right to give $20,000,000 as $20,000. If you have the right to give to one, you have the right to give to all; and, *as the Constitution neither defines charity nor stipulates the amount*, you are at liberty to give to any and everything which you may believe, or profess to believe, is a charity, and to any amount you may think proper. You will very easily perceive what a wide door this would open for fraud and corruption and favoritism, on the one hand, and for robbing the people on the other. No, Colonel, Congress has no right to give charity.

"Individual members may give as much of their own money as they please, but they have no right to touch a dollar of the public money for that purpose......There are plenty of wealthy men in and around Washington who could have given $20,000 without depriving themselves of even a luxury of life. The congressmen chose to keep their own money, which, if reports be true, some of them spend not very creditably; and the people about Washington , no doubt, applauded you for relieving them from the necessity of giving *by giving what was not yours to give.* The people have delegated to Congress, by the Constitution, the power to do certain things. To do these, it is authorized to collect and pay moneys, and for nothing else. Everything beyond this is usurpation, and a violation of the Constitution.

"'So you see, Colonel, you have violated the Constitution in what I consider a vital point. It is a precedent fraught with danger to the country, for when Congress once begins to stretch its power beyond the limits of the Constitution, there is no limit to it, and no security for the people..'"

(The anecdote continues for several more paragraphs, but the point is made.)

Notes and References

[1] Many Conservative pundits use the term "Socialism" to describe the current Obama / Democrat agenda. In truth, America has been on an increasingly socialistic path since the 1933 New Deal, regardless of whether Democrats or Republicans are in power. The term is incendiary but not very descriptive. We can better understand the term *Totalitarianism* by presenting governmental ideology as a spectrum or scale. At one end of this scale are minimalist intervention, maximum personal freedom and responsibility, and laisser-faire economic regulation. At the other extreme of the scale is absolute totalitarian government ownership and control of our property, our economic systems and businesses, our media, and our personal lives and decisions. An example of the former would be the early days of our country under the Articles of Confederation. Examples of the latter would be the Soviet Union in the 1930's or North Korea and Zimbabwe of today. Socialism, Communism, Dictatorship, Fascism, and Nazism are all descriptors of totalitarian governments, with the only difference being one of degree.

[2] Mark R. Levin, <u>On Liberty and Tyranny</u>, Threshold Editions, 2009

[3] Alexis de Tocqueville, <u>Democracy in America</u>, as quoted in Ibid, page 4

[4] U.S. Department of the Treasury, History of the U.S. Tax System, available at www.treasury.gov

[5] Amity Shlaes, <u>The Forgotten Man</u>, Harper Collins, 2007, page 11

6 Budget of the U.S. Government Historical Tables, Table 1.1, available at www.gpoaccess.gov

7 Marc Allen Eisner, <u>Regulatory Politics in Transition</u>, John Hopkins University Press, 2000 and
Gary Dean Best, <u>Pride, Prejudice and Politics: Roosevelt Versus Recovery 1933-1938</u>, Praeger Publishers, 1991

8 Amity Shlaes, <u>The Forgotten Man</u>, 2007, page 9

9 Walter Lippmann, The Conflict Within the New Deal, New York Herald Tribune, May 16, 1939, as reported on foxbusiness.com

10 Amity Shlaes, <u>The Forgotten Man</u>, 2007, page 9, And Robert S. McElvane, <u>The Great Depression</u>, Three Rivers Press, 1984, pages 307, 337

11 Amity Shlaes, <u>The Forgotten Man</u>, 2007, pages 7 and 9

12 Robert S. McElvane, <u>The Great Depression</u>, 1984, pages 329, 330

13 State of the Union Message to Congress, January 11, 1944, The American Presidency Project, available at www.presidency.ucsb.edu

14 Friedrich A. Hayek, <u>Road to Serfdom</u>, University of Chicago Press, 1944

15 Robert S. McElvane, <u>The Great Depression</u>, 1984, pages 333, 334 And Amity Shlaes, <u>The Forgotten Man</u>, 2007, page 11

[16] State of the Union Message to Congress, January 11, 1944, The American Presidency Project, available at www.presidency.ucsb.edu

[17] 41.5%. Congressional Budget Office, Budget Projections March 2010, Table 1-1, available at www.cbo.gov

[18] Congressional Budget Office, The Federal Budget Outlook Over the Long Run - June 2010, Box1-3, available at www.cbo.gov

[19] Niall Ferguson, How Great Powers Fall, Newsweek, December 7, 2009, page 41

[20] Congressional Budget Office, The Federal Budget Outlook Over the Long Run - June 2010, Box1-3, available at www.cbo.gov

[21] Budget of the U.S. Government Historical Tables, Table 1.1, available at www.gpoaccess.gov

[22] Ibid

[23] Congressional Budget Office, Budget and Economic Outlook - January 2010, Tables 1-3 & F-1, available at www.cbo.gov

[24] Congressional Budget Office, Budget and Economic Outlook 2010-2020, Table F-1, available at www.cbo.gov

[25] U.S. Treasury, Debt to the Penny, June 15, 2010, available at www.treasurydirect.gov

[26] Congressional Budget Office, Long Term Budget Scenarios, Figure 1-3, Alternative Fiscal Scenario, available at www.cbo.gov

[27] Congressional Budget Office, The Federal Budget Outlook Over the Long Run - June 2010, Figure1-3 and Page 16, available at www.cbo.gov

[28] Carmen Reinhart and Kenneth Rogoff, This Time is Different: A Panoramic View of Eight Centuries of Financial Crises, April 2008, available at www.economics.harvard.edu
And David R. Francis, An 800 Year History Lesson: big debts, long recovery, March 8, 2010, Christian Science Monitor, available at csmonitor.com

[29] U.S. Treasury, Debt to the Penny, June 15, 2010, available at www.treasurydirect.gov

[30] 2009 Social Security and Medicare Trustees Reports, as quoted by the National Center for Policy Analysis, Brief Analysis No. 662, June 11, 2009

[31] Congressional Budget Office, Baseline Budget Projections 2010-2020, Table 1-8, available at www.cbo.gov

[32] According to an interview with David Walker, former U.S. Comptroller General, with Patricia Murphy, correspondent for Politics Daily, on February 1, 2010, available at www.politicsdaily.com.

[33] Ibid

[34] Experian Global Press Office, Survey on Average Debt per Consumer, May 13, 2010, available at www.experian.com

[35] Gerald Prante, Tax Foundation, Summary of Latest Federal Individual Income Tax Data, Fiscal Fact No. 183, Table 1, available at www.taxfoundation.org

[36] Scott A. Hodge, Tax Foundation, Accounting for What Families Pay in Taxes and What They Receive in Government Spending, Fiscal Fact No. 189, available at www.taxfoundation.org

[37] William Beach, The 2009 Index of Dependence on Government, Heritage Foundation, March 2010, page 4, available at www.heritage.org

[38] Stephen Ohlemacher, Associated Press, Half of Households Don't Owe Uncle Sam, as reported in the Atlanta Journal Constitution, April 8, 2010

[39] Scott A. Hodge, Tax Foundation, Record Numbers of People Paying No Income Tax; Over 50 Million "Nonpayers" Include Families Making over $50,000, Fiscal Facts No. 214, available at www.taxfoundation.org

[40] According to an interview with David Walker, former U.S. Comptroller General, with Patricia Murphy, correspondent for Politics Daily, on February 1, 2010, available at www.politicsdaily.com.

[41] Elizabeth MacDonald, Tax Evasion, Corruption, and the European Bailout, May 27, 2010, available at www.emac.blogs.foxbusiness.com

[42] Social Security, Medicare and Medicaid spending totals approximately 40% of the current federal budget. Knight Kiplinger, A Stubborn U.S. Budget, Kiplinger's Personal Finance, August 2010 issue, page 19.

[43] Pamela Villarreal, National Center for Policy Analysis, Social Security and Medicare Projections: 2009, Brief Analysis No. 662, June 11, 2009

[44] Ibid

[45] 2009 Report of the Social Security and Medicare Trustees, available at www.ssa.gov

[46] William Beach, The 2009 Index of Dependence on Government, Heritage Foundation, March 2010, available at www.heritage.org

[47] Board of Governors of the Federal Reserve System, News and Events, Testimony April 14, 2010, available at www.federalreserve.gov

[48] Fox News, taken from Associated Press, Obama Signs $18 Billion Extension of Jobless Benefits, April 15, 2010, available at www.foxnews.com

[49] Jim Galloway, Political Insider, Atlanta Journal Constitution, April 14, 2010

[50] Kaiser Health News, Sebelius: Plan Coming to Reduce Minority Health Disparities, April 15, 2010, available at www.kaiserhealthnews.org

[51] William Beach, The 2009 Index of Dependence on Government, Heritage Foundation, March 2010, page 1, available at www.heritage.org

[52] Jill Jackson and John Nolen, CBS News Political Hotsheet, Health Care Reform Bill Summary, March 23, 2010, page 2, available at www.cbsnews.com

[53] William Beach, The 2009 Index of Dependence on Government, Heritage Foundation, March 2010, page 11, available at www.heritage.org

[54] Stephen Ohlemacher, Associated Press, Half of Households Don't Owe Uncle Sam, as reported in the Atlanta Journal Constitution, April 4, 2010

[55] William Beach, The 2009 Index of Dependence on Government, Heritage Foundation, March 2010, available at www.heritage.org

[56] David A. Patten, Newsmax, Heritage: Dependency on Government Skyrockets, June 28, 2010, available at www.newsmax.com

[57] William Beach, The 2009 Index of Dependence on Government, Page 6, Heritage Foundation, March 2010, available at www.heritage.org

[58] Robert Rector, Reducing Poverty by Revitalizing Marriage in Low-Income Communities, Heritage Foundation, January 2009, available at www.heritage.org

[59] William Beach and Patrick Tyrrell, The 2010 Index of Dependence on Government, Heritage Foundation, October 2010, Chart 4, available at www.heritage.org

[60] Isabel Sawhill and Ron Haskins (Co-directors of the Center on Children and Families at the Brooking Institution), Bad Economy Shakes American Myths, Atlanta Journal Constitution, November 5, 2009

[61] Ross Douthat, New York Time columnist, The American Family in Red, Blue, quoting a Pew Research Center study, as reported in the Atlanta Journal Constitution, May 13, 2010

[62] Robert Rector, Reducing Poverty by Revitalizing Marriage in Low-Income Communities, Heritage Foundation, January 2009, available at www.heritage.org

[63] As reported on WSB Radio, Atlanta GA, March 16, 2009

[64] Sheila M. Poole, Atlanta Marks National Day of Prayer Today, Atlanta Journal Constitution, May 6, 2010

[65] Newt Gingrich, Rediscovering God in America, Thomas Nelson, Inc., 2006

[66] Dr. Carol C. Adelman, Index of Global Philanthropy and Remittances 2010, The Center for Global Prosperity, The Hudson Institute, available at www.hudson.org, And Brett Schaefer, A Closer Look at American Generosity, January 2005, Heritage Foundation, available at www.heritage.org

[67] American Religious Identification Survey, 2008 Data Published by the U.S. Census Bureau, available at www.americanreligioussurevey-aris.org

[68] Ibid

69 National Cultural Values Survey, The Culture and Media Institute, available at www.cultureandmediainstitute.org

70 Pew Research Center, The Databank, Daily Number, available at www.pewresearch.org

71 Nathan Harden, Bawd and Man at Yale, National Review, April 5, 2010, page 26

72 Kathy Belge, Where Can Gays Legally Marry?, About.com - Lesbian Life, available at about.com

73 National Council on Economic Education, Understanding Economics in United States History, Visual 32.1, available at www.ushistory.councilforeconed.org

74 U.S. Bureau of Labor Statistics, Union Members Summary (USDL-10-0069), January 2010, available at www.data.bls.gov

75 Ibid

76 International Workers of the World, Celebrating Six Years of the IWW Starbucks Workers Union, June 9, 2010, available at www.iww.org

77 John Stossel, Southwest Sued Over Nursery Rhyme, ABC News 20/20, April 12, 2004, available at abcnews.go.com/2020

78 As reported in Q&A On The News, Atlanta Journal Constitution, May 10, 2010

79 Anne Flaherty, Graham Disinvited to Prayer Service, Associated Press, as reported in Atlanta Journal Constitution, April 23, 2010

80 Dr. Carol C. Adelman, Index of Global Philanthropy and Remittances 2010, The Center for Global Prosperity, The Hudson Institute, available at www.hudson.org, And Brett Schaefer, A Closer Look at American Generosity, January 2005, Heritage Foundation, available at www.heritage.org

81 Stephane Courtois, et al, The Black Book of Communism, page 9, Harvard University Press, 1999

82 Sewell Chan, Bank Tax Effort Sets Off Debate, New York Times, as reported in The Atlanta Journal Constitution, May 5, 2010

83 Elizabeth MacDonald, Wall Street Faces Broader Crackdown on Pay, October 1, 2010, available at www.foxbusines.com.

84 Michael Shear and Steven Mufson, Washington Post, June 5, 2010

85 As reported in the Atlanta Journal Constitution, June 7, 2010

86 Pew Research Center, Global Attitudes Project, Views of the Free Market, available at www.pewglobal.org

87 Aoife White and Robert Barr, British PM Has Somber Forecast, Associated Press, as reported in the Atlanta Journal Constitution, June 8, 2010

[88] David Stringer, Britain Raises Taxes, Slashes Its Spending, Associated Press, as reported in the Atlanta Journal Constitution, June 23, 2010

[89] Sarah Milov, Study Finds Academia May Favor Liberals, The Crimson (Harvard University Student Newspaper), April 7, 2005, available at www.thecrimson.com

[90] Patricia Cohen, Professor Is a Label That Leans to the Left, The New York Times, January 17, 2010, available at www.nytimes.com

[91] Tom Sabulis, Interview with Orit Sklar, June 27, 2010, The Atlanta Journal Constitution

[92] Congressional Budget Office, The Budget and Economic Outlook (January 2010), Table F-1 Revenues, Outlays, Deficits, Surpluses and Debt Held By the Public, 1970 to 2009. available at www.cbo.gov

[93] Pew Research Center for the People and the Press, Distrust, Discontent, Anger and Partisan Rancor, April 18, 2010, available at www.pewresearch.org

[94] Endangered Species Act, available at www.Encyclopedia Brittanica.com, And
Jonathan Adler, Bad For Your Land, Bad For The Critters, Wall Street Journal, December 31, 2003, And
Valerie Richardson, It's Farmers vs. Fish For California Water, Washington Times, August 20, 2009, available at www.washingtontimes.com

[95] Statistics from 1973 and 2006: Center for Public Integrity, Foreign Oil Dependence Has Grown, available at www.publicintegrity.org

2008 data and Historical Graph: DOE Energy Information Administration, Independent Statistics and Analysis, Petroleum Navigator, available at www.eia.doe.gov

[96] DOE Energy Information Administration, Independent Statistics and Analysis, Energy in Brief, How Dependent Are We On Foreign Oil, available at www.eia.doe.gov

[97] U.S. Department of Energy website, www.energy.gov

[98] Energy Department Fails Its Own Audit, Wall Street Journal, June 8, 2009, available at www.wsj.com

[99] Sean Paige, Energy Failure, Insight on the News, July 17, 200, available at www.findarticles.com

[100] U.S. Department of Energy website, www.energy.gov

[101] Incinerating Cash, The Department of Energy's Failure to Develop and Use Innovative Technologies To Clean Up the Nuclear Waste Legacy, Staff Report for the Committee on Energy and Commerce, October 2000, available at www.mindfully.org

[102] U.S. Department of Energy website, Documents and Publications. GAO Reports, available at www.energy.gov

[103] U.S. Department of Energy website, www.energy.gov

[104] Mark R. Levin, Liberty and Tyranny, 2009, pages 68-72

[105] According to segment from Special Report with Britt Hume, Fox News Channel, September 24, 2008

[106] As of June 2010, the two GSE's had borrowed $145 Billion. The Congressional Budget Office has estimated they will need $389 Billion through 2019. The One Trillion worst case scenario was estimated by Sean Egan, a respected investment adviser. All as reported in: Woellert and Gittelsohn, Fannie-Freddie Fix at $160 Billion With $1 Trillion Worst Case, Bloomberg News, June 13, 2010, available at www.bloomberg.com

[107] Joint Economic Committee of the U.S. Congress, Are Health Care Reform Cost Estimates Accurate?, July 31, 2009, available at www.jec.senate.gov

[108] 2009 Report of the Social Security and Medicare Trustees, available at www.ssa.gov

[109] Ibid

[110] Jill Jackson and John Nolen, CBS News Political Hotsheet, Health Care Reform Bill Summary, March 23, 2010, page 1, available at www.cbsnews.com

[111] There may not be definitive, comprehensive, unbiased and uncontested documentation on the net costs of governmental services consumed or required by illegal immigrants at the federal, state, and local level. There have been many estimates by various groups. Immigration control groups produce very large numbers. One such estimate exceeded $300 Billion, but included such claims as "suppressed wages". Not surprisingly, immigration advocacy groups produce smaller numbers or even contend that the taxes paid by illegals are higher than the services they consume. This is unlikely. The very nature of the shadow world they inhabit makes accuracy difficult. A study by the University of Arizona, (Conn Carroll, Illegal

Immigration Costs Demonstrated Again, March 6, 2008, available at www.heritage.org) found that *counties* along the Mexican Border spend over $1 Billion processing illegals through their legal system each year. The same report quoted Heritage research which shows that the net cost for local governments to provide education, welfare and criminal justice, after taxes paid are subtracted, is $8,800 per household per year, which would put the total cost to *local* government well into the billions. The Washington Post reported a study by the Center for Immigration Studies that put the net cost to the *federal* government at $10.4 Billion (Mary Fitzgerald, Illegal Immigrants Cost to Government Studied, August 26, 2004, available at www.washingtonpost.com). Another study by the Federation for American Immigration Reform estimated the cost to the *State* of California to be $10.5 Billion per year in health care and education (Robert Longley, State's Cheap Labor Costs Average Household $1,183 a Year, December 2004, available at usgovinfo.about.com). The same group estimated the cost to the *State* of Arizona was $2.7 Billion per year (Ed Barnes, Cost of Illegal Immigration Rising Rapidly in Arizona, Study Finds, Fox News, May 17, 2010, available at www.foxnews.com). We may not know an exact cost, but we know the cost is large and growing.

112 If there is any doubt about this in the reader's mind, simply look at the labels in virtually any retail store, examine the Spanish language forms available from almost every governmental agency website (including the IRS), or call the main phone line of virtually any large company to hear an option for "en Espanol".

113 Henry Steele Commager, Editor, Illustrated History of the Civil War, Promontory Press, 1976

114 U.S. National Archives, Combat Area Casualty File, available at www.archives.gov

115 CBS News, Iraq War's Price Tag Nears Vietnams', July 25, 2008, available at www.cbsnews.com

116 Ray Bonds, Editor, <u>The Vietnam War, The Illustrated History of the Conflict in Southeast Asia</u>, Crown Publishers, 1979

117 Tax Foundation, State Individual Income Tax Rates As of February 2010, available at www.taxfoundation.org

118 Tax Foundation, 2010 Facts and Figures, available at www.taxfoundation.org

119 Ibid

120 U.S. Census 2010 Statistical Abstract, Table 431 and Table 12, available at www.census.gov

121 George Will, California a Good Example of How Government Goes Bad, as posted in the Atlanta Journal Constitution, May 3, 2009

122 California Health Care Foundation Almanac, September 2009, available at www.chcf.org

123 Budget Deal Brings Sales Tax Increase, Atlanta Journal Constitution, February 20, 2009

124 New York Times, California Budget Crisis, January 7, 2010, available at www.nytimes.com

[125] Wall Street Journal, California Stealin', November 4, 2009

[126] New York Times, California Budget Crisis, January 7, 2010, available at www.nytimes.com

[127] Randal C. Archibold, California, in Financial Crisis, Opens Prison Doors, New York Times, March 23, 2010, available at www.nytimes.com

[128] Tax Foundation, State Comparisons of Corporate Taxes, available at www.taxfoundation.org

[129] Website of State Senator Dave Cogdill, The Numbers: California in Bad Shape, quoting an article in the San Diego Business Tribune and other sources, August 8, 2008, available at www.cssrc.us

[130] U.S. Department of Labor, Bureau of Labor Statistics, State Unemployment Summary, available at www.bls.gov

[131] RealtyTrac, State Foreclosures, available at www.realtytrac.com

[132] California EPA Air Resources Board, Fact Sheets: Climate Change Emissions Control Regulations, and Climate Change AB 32 Scoping Plan, available at www.arb.ca.gov

[133] Peter Henderson, California Sees Big Costs to Renewable Power Plan, Reuters News Service, June 12, 2009

[134] U.S. Department of Education, Institute of Education Sciences, National Center for Education Statistics,

Snapshot State Report 2009: Grade 4 Math scores were lower in only 3 other states. Only 30% of students scored as Proficient. Grade 4 Reading scores were lower in only 1 other state. Only 24% of students scored as Proficient. Grade 8 Math scores were lower in only 2 other states. Only 23% of students scored as Proficient. Grade 8 Reading scores were lower in only 1 other state. Only 22% of students scored as Proficient. Available at www.nces.ed.gov

[135] National Education Association, Rankings and Estimates 2008, Table 1 Average Salaries, available at www.nea.org

[136] Catherine Rampell, New York Times, Of All States, New York Schools Spend Most Money Per Pupil, Figure 4: Current Spending Amounts by State, July 27, 2009, available at www.economix.blogs.nytimes.com

[137] Education Data Partnership, Comparing California June 2008, available at www.ed-data.k12.ca.us

[138] California Department of Education, Educational Demographics Unit, Data Quest, Statewide Enrollment by Ethnicity 2008-2009, Students by Learner in Another Language, Teachers Providing Services to English Learners, available at www.dq.cde.ca.gov

[139] Benjamin Schwarz, California Dreamers, The Atlantic (Magazine), July/August 2009, available at www.theatlantic.com

[140] Public Policy Institute of California, Just The Facts, Illegal Immigrants, June 2008, available at www.ppic.org

141 American Legislative Exchange Council, Rich States Poor States, available at www.alec.org

142 Morley Winograd and Michael D. Hais (co-authors of the book Millennial Makeover: MySpace, YouTube, and the Future of American Politics), GOP Tone Deaf to Generation That Will Shape Politics, Atlanta Journal Constitution, May 14, 2009

143 Pew Research Center, The Millennials: Confident. Connected. Open to Change, February 24, 2010, available at www.pewresearch.org

144 Saul D. Alinsky, Rules for Radicals: A Practical Primer for Realistic Radicals, Random House, 1971

145 Gallup, In 2010, Conservatives Still Outnumber Moderates, Liberals, June 25, 2010, available at www.gallup.com

146 CNN Chief: Others Not Airing News Without Bias, Atlanta Journal Constitution, April 15, 2010

147 Circulation Declines Persist at Newspapers, October 27, 2009; and Top Papers' Circulation Drops, April 27, 2010, both as reported in the Atlanta Journal Constitution

148 Pew Research Center for the People and the Press, Press Accuracy Rating Hits Two Decade Low, Public Evaluations of the News Media: 1985-2009, available at www.people-press.org

149 73% felt people should produce documents verifying legal status. Considering everything, 59% approved of new Arizona law. Pew Research Center for People and the

Press, Broad Approval for New Arizona Immigration Law, May 12, 2010, available at www.people-press.org

[150] Please refer back to Footnote 111

[151] John P. Avalon, What Independent Voters Want, The Wall Street Journal, October 20, 2008, available at www.wsj.com; And, Emily Smith, What Independent Voters Want in 2010, The Weekly Standard, September 15, 2009, available at www.weeklystandard.com

[152] Foundation for Economic Education, available at www.fee.org

Made in the USA
Charleston, SC
06 February 2011